A VILLAGE DESTROYED

MAY 14, 1999

Note on names: First mention of all place names in
Kosovo is provided in both the Serbian and Albanian
languages. Thereafter, for the sake of simplicity and
consistency, and in conformity with English-language
practice, all names are in Serbian.

Some of the names of individuals in the book have
been changed to protect them from possible retaliations
and further hardship.

Human Rights Watch

Human Rights Center
University of California, Berkeley

University of California Press
Berkeley and Los Angeles, California

University of California Press, Ltd.
London, England

Manufactured in Italy
10 09 08 07 06 05 04 03 02
10 9 8 7 6 5 4 3 2 1

The paper used in this publication meets the minimum
requirements of ANSI/NISO Z39.48-1992 (R 1997)
(Permanence of Paper).

Library of Congress Cataloging-in-Publication Data

Abrahams, Fred.

A village destroyed, May 14, 1999 : war crimes in Kosovo
/ text, Fred Abrahams and Eric Stover ; photographs,
Gilles Peress ; introduction, Carroll Bogert.

    p. cm.

Includes bibliographical references.

ISBN 0-520-23302-6 (alk. paper). — ISBN 0-520-23303-4
(alk. paper)

1. Kosovo (Serbia)—History—Civil War, 1998—Atrocities.
2. Albanians—Crimes against—Yugoslavia—Kosovo (Serbia)
I. Title: War crimes in Kosovo. II. Stover, Eric. III. Peress,
Gilles. IV. Title.

DR2087.6.A78 A25 2001

949.7109—dc21   2001042309

A VILLAGE DESTROYED
MAY 14, 1999

War Crimes
in Kosovo

TEXT: FRED ABRAHAMS AND ERIC STOVER
PHOTOGRAPHS: GILLES PERESS
INTRODUCTION: CARROLL BOGERT
DESIGN: GILLES PERESS AND JEFF STREEPER
PROJECT COORDINATION: LISA USDAN

HUMAN RIGHTS WATCH

HUMAN RIGHTS CENTER AT
UNIVERSITY OF CALIFORNIA, BERKELEY

UNIVERSITY OF CALIFORNIA PRESS
BERKELEY, LOS ANGELES, LONDON

CONTENTS

INTRODUCTION

TEXT BY
CARROLL BOGERT

When NATO went to war over Kosovo in 1999, there was no traditional battlefield. The Atlantic allies fought entirely from the skies. Their enemies, the Yugoslav army, Serbian police and paramilitaries, mostly attacked civilians – a cruel specialty they had honed over the past decade in Bosnia and Croatia. Journalists had no real theater of combat to cover, no frontlines to follow on a map, no advances and retreats to pursue. With a few exceptions, outsiders had virtually no access to the war on the ground in Kosovo.

Human Rights Watch published its first report about Kosovo in 1990, and went on to document the Serbian government's stranglehold on the region in many dispatches over the next decade. Its last report before the NATO bombing began, *A Week of Terror in Drenica*, published in February 1999, gave evidence of the growing seriousness of war crimes in Kosovo. The report helped to prompt the feeling, among European and American politicians, that something had to be done.

When the war finally broke out, Human Rights Watch's researchers were as eager as the journalists to uncover what was happening inside Kosovo. There were three options, all of them unsatisfactory in some degree. The first was to be based in Belgrade, which was the target of many NATO air strikes and the source of highly unreliable information about casualties suffered throughout the country, including Kosovo. The second was to sit in Brussels, a source of more reliable, but still incomplete, information from the NATO high command. And the third was to scramble along the borders of Kosovo, mostly in Albania and Macedonia, where hundreds of thousands of Kosovar Albanians were pouring across, traumatized, exhausted, and in fear for their lives.

The third option, in the end, produced the best reporting about what was really happening in Kosovo. From these terrorized refugees came surprisingly detailed accounts of the atrocities they were fleeing. When, after the war, researchers and reporters rushed into Kosovo, they found a chillingly accurate *nature morte*: almost invariably, the dead bodies were just where the refugees said they'd be. And the torched houses were exactly the same houses that refugees said were set on fire.

The fact that these testimonial accounts matched the facts on the ground so closely is highly significant. Governments engaged in massive human rights abuse often claim, when presented with the accounts of victims and eyewitnesses, that such sources are unreliable. These people fled the scene, they can't remember what happened, they're hysterical, they're politicized, they can't be trusted. But when enough people are interviewed, and their accounts are cross-checked with care, a true picture of events can emerge. This methodology carried the day in Kosovo, where so many people who gathered information on the border were able, not long after, to enter Kosovo itself and check out the refugees' stories. To a surprising degree, the stories were confirmed.

This is the new face of war reporting in our times. Whether it's Kosovo, Chechnya, or Sierra Leone, actual fighting between armies can be hard to observe. The only immediate sources of information are the civilian victims and witnesses, who escape the conflict and give their accounts to human rights workers and journalists.

This kind of reporting requires a skilled researcher with the patience to interview a large number of refugees, to weed out the wild or inflated tales, to speak to victims separately and corroborate their stories, and to comb refugee camps for multiple witnesses from a single village or a single region. It takes time. In an era when media budgets for international news are being slashed, it takes resources. And in an era when news is becoming entertainment and the public is presumed not to want to hear about the atrocities suffered by a faraway people, it takes the courage to say: this matters. This story is worth getting.

2

The war in Kosovo was a turning point for Human Rights Watch. Over its twenty-year history, the organization had documented many wars and internal conflicts. But often those reports were written later, after the fighting had ended. For the first time, over the many weeks of the NATO bombing campaign, human rights researchers were sending out fast dispatches based on refugee accounts and sources inside Kosovo – applying the same painstaking methodology of traditional human rights work, but at a breakneck pace. Modern technology, of course, made this possible. Cell phones and satellite phones and emails and web postings got the information out of the Balkan countryside and into the headquarters of Human Rights Watch in New York, where, after being analyzed, it was sent on to the media, the policymakers, and the general public.

This book tells the story of how Kosovar Albanians were exiled from their homeland, and how they returned. It recounts the destruction of one village in Kosovo, and how modern technology enabled a human rights researcher to piece together the facts of what happened. It describes how photographs of Serb paramilitaries were downloaded onto a laptop and carried into a decimated Kosovo village where cows wandered among the ruins, and how survivors, gaping at pixels on a screen, recognized and identified their attackers, beyond a shadow of a doubt. Technology enabled a new kind of human rights reporting from Kosovo, one that was fast and decisive. It also gave that information a bigger punch.

Human rights reporting is changing in the age of international war crimes tribunals. The United Nations established the International Criminal Tribunal for the former Yugoslavia in 1993, and while the NATO bombing was underway, the Tribunal's chief prosecutor indicted Slobodan Milosevic, then President of Serbia, for his crimes in Kosovo. Before long, an International Criminal Court will have the authority, at least in theory, to judge very serious human rights crimes that take place anywhere in the world. Human rights reports have always been intended to inform the public, to shame the perpetrator, and to put the truth on record. Now they could actually help put someone in jail.

The book you hold in your hands is not just a piece of journalism, and it's not just a human rights report. It's a piece of documentary evidence. Read it, look at it, and judge for yourself.

"If you seek vengeance, dig two graves."
—Chinese Proverb

The photo essay by Gilles Peress entitled "Exile and Return" was originally commissioned by *The New Yorker* magazine and published in its July 19, 1999, issue.

EXILE AND RETURN

TEXT BY
ERIC STOVER
PHOTOGRAPHS BY
GILLES PERESS

As the mist slowly lifted one April morning, we watched as thousands of refugees, their faces blistered by the sun and wind, streamed into the Morina borderpost in northern Albania.

It was the spring of 1999, and Yugoslav troops and Serb police were sweeping through Kosovo forcing more than 800,000 ethnic Albanians to flee their homes. They were victims of a crime against humanity, the largest single eviction of a civilian population in Europe since 1945.

EXILE

He emerged from the mist of no-man's land, a hundred meters away from where we stood on the Albanian side of the border. A middle-aged, heavy-set man in a bulky gray sweater, he looked agitated, his body swaying, his hands shaking, unsure of what to do next. Someone appeared at his side: a Serb military policeman, judging by his blue uniform. The policeman moved behind the man, raised his arm, and shouted something. The man lurched forward like a puppet and fell to his knees. Finding his footing again, he stood up and ran across the stone bridge to the red gates of Morina.

The man struggled to catch his breath as he spoke. His name was Sefer Hoxha. Just before daybreak, three Serb military policemen had come to his home in Prizren, he said. They had stormed through the house, ripping open mattresses and emptying drawers onto the floor, looking for jewelry and money. They forced Sefer and his oldest son, Hamit, into a jeep and drove them to the police station. After an hour, Hamit was taken away, and Sefer was bundled into the jeep and driven to the border.

On the road leaving Prizren, Sefer saw thousands of people on both sides of the highway. Some were in cars, but most were on foot, squatting together in family groups, or resting on tractors or wooden hay carts heaped with household wares. Serb policemen moved down the column, demanding documents and money. At the end of the line, next to the border hut, he saw two guards pulling off license plates with pliers and pitching them into the bed of a pickup truck. As Sefer completed his story, someone handed him a water bottle. He took two swallows, then turned to his side and retched.

It was a stifling hot day in mid-April, three weeks after NATO had begun its bombing campaign over Yugoslavia. Hundreds of thousands of Kosovar Albanians like Sefer Hoxha had already been forced by Serbian troops and paramilitaries to flee their homes. They were victims of a crime against humanity, the largest single eviction of a civilian population in Europe since 1945. When interviewed on Serbian television, President Slobodan Milosevic denied playing any role in the expulsions. The Kosovars, like the birds, he said, were fleeing NATO bombs. Few foreign journalists or human rights investigators could get into Kosovo to investigate Milosevic's claim. Instead, they had to wait at border crossings like Morina to gather accounts from the refugees themselves.

Kosovo had always been a seedbed of Serb nationalism and a place of occasional but bloody clashes between Serbs and Albanians. In the Yugoslavia of Marshal Tito, Kosovo was a self-governing province, and Kosovars of all ethnicities enjoyed substantial autonomy. Tito's brand of "socialism and brotherhood" kept ethnic relations in the province relatively civil and peaceful. After Tito's death in 1980, and the rise of nationalism throughout the former Yugoslavia, Kosovar Serbs began to protest discrimination at the hands of the ethnic Albanian authorities. Albanians comprised approximately 85 percent of Kosovo's population. As Slobodan Milosevic climbed the political ranks in the late 1980s, from head of the communist party in Belgrade to President of Serbia, he seized on these grievances, as well as the centuries-old myth of Kosovo as the Serbian heartland, to create an image of himself as the defender of Serbian minorities throughout Yugoslavia. In 1989 Milosevic abolished Kosovo's autonomy, re-asserted Serbian direct rule, and purged ethnic Albanians from jobs in government and education. Kosovar Albanians were prohibited from buying or selling property without permission, and sales of property to Albanians by departing Serbs were annulled. A powerful police presence enforced Belgrade's control. Kosovar Albanians responded by declaring an independent state and establishing their own parallel structures. They elected a parliament, collected funds to pay for schools and health care, and refused to take part in Serbian elections.

By 1997, Kosovo had become a tinderbox. The Serb police—MUP—were responsible for serious human rights violations, including illegal detentions, beatings, and torture. Political trials were commonplace. Meanwhile, Albanians were growing increasingly restless and frustrated that their peaceful resistance was not bearing fruit. A small militant group called the Kosovo Liberation Army (KLA; in Albanian, Ushtria Clirimtare e Kosoves or UCK), formed in the early 1990s, began to attack police stations with greater frequency. The police responded with indiscriminate and excessive force, which swelled the ranks of the nascent insurgency. By 1998, the KLA was gaining control in parts of the Kosovar countryside, kidnapping and killing Serb civilians and ambushing Serb patrols. The government's retaliation was fierce. The Serbian police and later Yugoslav Army swept through villages thought to be harboring KLA guerrillas, destroying homes and burning crops. By mid-October 1998, over 298,000 Kosovars—approximately 15 percent of the population—had been displaced within Kosovo or had left the province.

In early 1999, as fighting intensified between the KLA and Yugoslav forces, Milosevic stepped up his assault on Kosovar Albanians. He placed his forces—regular soldiers, the blue-uniformed Special Police of the Interior Ministry and the dreaded private armies of ultra-nationalist warlords—under a single command. Their purpose was twofold: crushing the KLA and permanently changing the ethnic balance of Kosovo by driving out as many ethnic Albanians as possible.

The "campaign of terror," as the International Criminal Tribunal for the former Yugoslavia later labeled the operation, was fueled by the most potent of human cleansers: fear. Once word traveled up a valley that Serb police and paramilitary units had begun pillaging and burning a particular village, panic would sweep from one hamlet to another as inhabitants rushed to gather their families together and flee.

By noon on the day Sefer Hoxha crossed to safety, the Morina borderpost was overrun by refugees. On the lighter days, when only a few hundred refugees had reached the crossing, the Albanian border guards had little trouble containing the arriving crowds. The guards sat at a small wooden table, blue hats pushed back on their foreheads, shouting for order as they questioned each family group, noting the name of the head of household, place of residence, and number of family members. But today was different. In the five hours since Sefer had crossed the border, more than ten thousand people had surged through the gates. By nightfall, twice as many more refugees would pour across the border with thousands more still waiting to get in.

The flows, rivers, floods of people that crossed over Kosovo's border in the spring of 1999 caught international aid organizations unprepared and ill-equipped to respond to the crisis. In the end, it was NATO that took care of most of the refugees. Only a military organization of such size had the money, logistical capability, and political muscle to build and maintain camps for hundreds of thousands. Nowhere was this more evident than in the Albanian town of Kukes, located 16 kilometers down a dirt road from the Morina crossing. An impoverished town frequently buffeted by freezing winds and surrounded by rugged mountains, Kukes was not the best location for a refugee camp. Treacherous roads hampered the delivery of aid to Kukes, and relief organizations had to rely on NATO transport planes and helicopters to ferry in food and supplies.

9

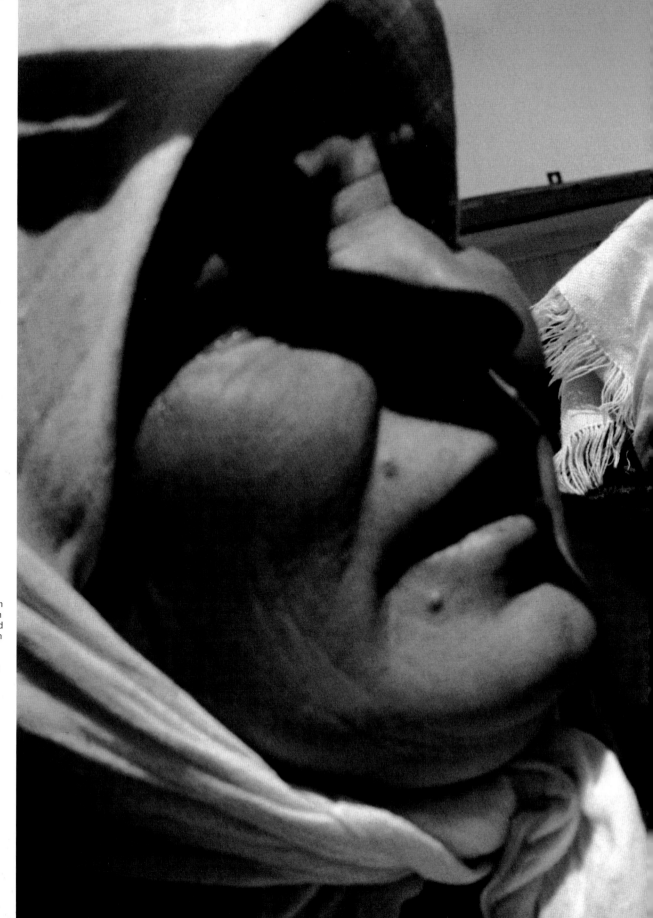

Forced to leave their men behind, Kosovar Albanian women in a tractor-pulled cart trundled into exile in northern Albania at the Morina border crossing, where tens of thousands of refugees arrived each day during the mass expulsions in late March and early April 1999.

By mid-April, Kukes was overflowing with more than 300,000 refugees. The town's playing field, theaters, and parking lots had been converted into makeshift camps. A few refugees were housed with town residents, but the vast majority lived in tent camps, which the spring rains had turned into muddy quagmires rampant with dysentery. The most squalid camp could be found on the grounds of an abandoned potato factory. Eight hundred refugees had occupied the factory itself, with fifty or more people crammed into each room. The building's lower floors were used as open latrines and the stench wafted out onto the factory's parking lot where thousands more huddled under makeshift tents constructed from scraps of wood and plastic sheeting. At dusk, a green truck would cruise through, and aid workers would toss out vegetables and loaves of bread as children ran after the truck fighting for every scrap of food.

It is hard to convey what it is like to watch over 23,000 people converge on an isolated border station in a single day. One thinks of images from the "Trail of Tears" in the winter of 1838–39, when the U.S. government, in its campaign to open land to white settlement in the southeastern United States, forced 16,000 Cherokee Indians (of which 4,000 died of cold, hunger, and disease) to flee to western lands. Or the Spanish Civil War in the 1930s, when some 400,000 civilians crossed into France in ten days. Or the scorched-earth campaign of the Guatemalan generals in the 1980s that sent tens of thousands of Mayan Indians fleeing to southern Mexico. But like all things in history, such events soon become nothing more than vague abstractions, flattened by the ambiguity of words and the nullity of numbers.

Morina, like other "refugee influx points" (as the United Nations High Commissioner for Refugees referred to them), had little to offer people once they crossed into Albanian territory. Two aid organizations—Catholic Relief Services (CRS) and the French-based Medecins du Monde (MDM)—worked valiantly to feed and care for those most in need. Young CRS workers in T-shirts and faded blue jeans, their heads wrapped in brightly colored kerchiefs, would hand out fruit and bottled water. It was a simple gesture, but one that brought enormous relief to the terrified refugees. In response to cries for medical help, doctors with Medecins du Monde would swoop into the crowd with green stretchers and carry the sick and wounded to hospital tents they had set up just out of Serb gunshot range. Dozens of foreign journalists and a handful of investigators, myself included, circulated through the crowds seeking interviews, which most people were eager to give.

Human rights documentation during armed conflicts is essentially collecting the accounts of war crimes—preferably as soon after they occur as possible—from victims and witnesses and then investigating their veracity. Informants, no matter how well-intentioned, can often exaggerate or omit important details. This is why it is important to cross-check accounts with as many witnesses as possible. Documenting what are essentially indictable criminal actions also means researchers must have a firm grasp of international humanitarian law as codified in the 1949 Geneva Conventions and the two Additional Protocols of 1977 or, as the military prefers, the laws of war.

Often the best single indicator of a major war crime is a massive displacement of civilians. But even that phenomenon can be deceptive. People may flee for their lives because of the intensity of the fighting or because their leaders ordered them out. They may be fleeing because they and their leaders have committed massive crimes and fear retribution. Or, as Milosevic was claiming in Kosovo, people were fleeing en masse because of NATO bombs. Determinations such as these, especially when direct access to an armed conflict is so restricted, are hard to make in the best of circumstances.

Over the past two decades, researchers from the New York–based Human Rights Watch have become a vigilant presence in war zones around the world. The human rights group dispatched its first investigator to Morina on March 28, four days after the NATO bombing had begun. Other researchers soon followed, and by mid-June, the organization had gathered hundreds of testimonies from refugees at nearly every major border crossing on Kosovo's western and southern frontiers. Accounts of some large-scale atrocities were often fragmentary at best and, before being made public, required further investigation and verification. In Montenegro, for instance, Human Rights Watch researcher Bogdan Ivanisevic interviewed two women who reported a massacre of over forty men at the hands of Serbian troops and paramilitaries in their village of Cuska (Qyshk in Albanian). It was the kind of story that would make headlines in major newspapers worldwide. But when Ivanisevic questioned the women further, he learned that they had been expelled from the village moments before the killings took place. Not having actual eyewitnesses of the alleged massacre gave Ivanisevic and his colleagues in New York pause and they decided to investigate the incident further before releasing it publicly.

One of those fortunate enough to escape the war in Kosovo was 19-year-old Leonora Lutolli. Rail thin, with bleach blond hair and large brown eyes, Leonora arrived in Morina on the evening of March 29 with her mother and younger sister. A week earlier, Leonora and Adrianna, her best friend, had been having coffee at a bar in Pristina when a burst of bullets tore through the window. Adrianna was killed instantly; Leonora was knocked unconscious, but survived with bullet fragments embedded in her arm and neck. After she was released from the hospital, Leonora and her family fled to the Albanian border. From Morina, the Albanian authorities transported Leonora and her family to Kukes and then on to a village in the interior of the country. A week later, bored and restless, she caught a bus to the Albanian capital of Tirana, where I met her through a mutual acquaintance and hired her to work as my interpreter.

The day before the huge influx of refugees began, Leonora had noticed two boys at the Morina gates, their hands gripping the railing as they stared intently at the wall of humanity approaching them. Occasionally, the taller boy, who was dressed in a faded 101 Dalmatians T-shirt and baggy jeans, would stand on his tiptoes and point at someone in the crowd. When he realized that it wasn't the person he was looking for, he would let his arm go limp and once again press his forehead against the gate. Eleven days earlier, they told us, a Serb policeman had stopped the boys on their way to buy bread in their hometown of Prizren and put them on a bus bound for the Morina crossing. They now lived at the borderpost, surviving on handouts from the aid workers and journalists. Morning after morning they would appear at the gates to wait in vain for their parents to arrive.

On most mornings the two boys were joined by a young man dressed in a light green ski jacket and faded jeans. His name was Faton "Toni" Preteni and, like the boys, he was waiting for his parents to emerge from the column of people crossing the border. Fluent in English, he had found work translating for a CNN crew. Every evening, as the crew packed up its equipment, they asked Toni if he would return with them to Kukes. But he always refused, preferring to sleep in the open or, when it rained, in an abandoned car a few hundred yards from the border crossing. Seeing how bedraggled he looked one morning, I gave him my sleeping bag, which he promptly handed over to the two boys.

Before the war, Toni had been employed as a driver for the Organization for Security and Cooperation in Europe (OSCE) in his hometown of Mitrovica (Mitrovice), an industrial city in northern Kosovo. In 1998, after more than six months of intense fighting between the KLA and

Some refugees arrived at the border crossing in cars, but most came on foot or on tractors and wooden hay carts heaped with household wares. They told of Serb police and militiamen at checkpoints demanding money and documents before allowing the refugees through to the border.

Yugoslav forces, the UN Security Council passed a resolution calling for an immediate cease-fire and for the deployment of an international presence to monitor it. Soon thereafter, OSCE monitors were deployed across Kosovo. They stayed there until the eve of the NATO strikes in mid-March. The evening that the OSCE began withdrawing its personnel, Toni was told to go to his boss's house and to drive him to headquarters. But, as he approached the house, two Serb policemen stopped him and demanded money. When Toni refused, one of the policemen pulled a grenade from his belt and motioned as if he were going to toss it on the car. Toni pressed hard on the accelerator and sped away. When the NATO strikes began, Toni left Mitrovica with his mother and father and walked to a nearby village where his uncle lived. They had been there a week when his father and mother returned to Mitrovica to refill her prescription for a heart ailment. The next day, Yugoslav troops attacked the village, and Toni and his uncle fled to the border.

Weeks later, after I had returned to the United States, I received a phone call from Toni. He was still in Morina, he said, working with another TV crew. "Guess what?" he asked, barely able to contain himself. "My parents have arrived!" I congratulated him and then asked what had happened to the two boys. There was a pause on the line and when Toni's voice came back it was fainter. "They're still here, waiting," he said. "But I don't know. It doesn't look so good."

As thousands and thousands of refugees streamed across the border, the scene at Morina became more chaotic. The stench of vomit and urine stung the air. At one point, the influx of refugees reached such a frenzied pitch that the border guards abandoned their record-keeping, snatched up the table, and fled to the customs hut. Gusts of wind would sweep across the border station flicking grains of sand like a thousand knives into whatever or whomever stood in their path. At times, when NATO bombers swept low over the crest of hills, the Serbs would suddenly stop the flow of refugees and the incessant rumbling of tractor engines would be replaced by the sound of children sobbing and the rustling of plastic sheeting. There were even moments of bitter comedy. When an old man dressed in the traditional white, conical hat called a *qeleshe* wheeled his sleeping wife through the gates in a rickety wheelbarrow and sensed he had an audience, he lifted his hands into the air, upending both the wheelbarrow and his wife, as he shouted: "They took it all! Even my wedding ring! The bastards!"

More is lost than gained when listening to the stories of refugees. The eye can never register every nuance in the storyteller's face, nor can the ear discern every subtle shift in emotion, nor the hand move quickly enough to capture in print every word. Most stories never make it into print, let alone into a courtroom. They lie buried in notebooks, only to be recounted in the starkest terms or perhaps never to be told again.

Almost all refugees had lost something during their flight from Kosovo that spring of 1999. Be it a house. Or an entire life's savings. Or a loved one. As I listened to some of their accounts, I could feel the slipstream of vengeance tugging at their words or even flashing to the surface. "What did I lose?" an old man barked back at me as he raised his finger to my face. "My dignity!" Then, gripping my shoulder with his other hand, he added: "And, believe me, someone will pay for that!"

"The police took my tractor," a man in thick black glasses and a heavy beard told me. "It was a red International and had a silver horseshoe on front. Do you know how long I saved so I could buy that tractor? Eighteen long years. And they took it just because of my last name." For farmers in Kosovo—or for all of the southern Balkans, for that matter—a tractor was a prized possession, which explained why there were so many of them parked in the camps. "Only death will separate me from my tractor," another refugee told me at the border. When I saw him later that evening in Kukes, I found that he had used scraps of wood and plastic sheeting to construct a makeshift tent over his tractor. Below the engine mount, stretched out asleep, were his wife and three children. "This is our only home now," he said. "And it will be our last one."

Qerim Tahi, a 46-year-old teacher from Ladrovic (Ladroviq), and his wife, Hajrie, said Serb soldiers and paramilitaries in light green uniforms stopped them and others at a checkpoint near the town of Malisevo (Malisheve). As I interviewed the couple, three teenage girls, wrapped in blankets, hovered just within earshot. That night, Qerim said, the militiamen forced the people from their carts and ordered them to kneel on the ground. Cradling AK-47 assault rifles, the militiamen moved systematically along the line, ordering the women to drop their jewelry on the ground and the men to empty their pockets. The paramilitaries scooped up rings, bracelets, passports, drivers licenses, pocket watches, pen knives, photographs, and Deutschmarks and tossed them into a large burlap bag. Qerim paused and gestured to the three girls. "The [militiamen] forced these girls to undress in front of everyone and then humiliated them. It was like they were playing a game." Qerim put his hand on the shoulder of one of the girls, a redhead with a large purple welt just above her right eye. "This one," he said. "She's tough. She refused to strip, so one of the militiamen struck her with the butt of his rifle."

As with all wars, there is no way of knowing how many women were raped or abused during their flight from Kosovo in the spring of 1999. Victims of sexual abuse often are reluctant to talk about what happened to them either because they fear further abuse or are ashamed, or because they dread the possibility that they may be shunned by their families and communities. Rape is a deeply sensitive subject in ethnic Albanian communities in Kosovo, a largely traditional society, where a sexual assault can permanently stigmatize a woman, shaming her family and ruining her marriage or prospects for marriage. Gathering firsthand accounts of rape proved difficult for human rights researchers and journalists. Nevertheless, interviews with hundreds of women make clear that sexual violence was common during the war in Kosovo. Joanne Mariner of Human Rights Watch, for example, after interviewing over a dozen ethnic Albanian women at the Morina crossing, concluded that Serb troops had captured and repeatedly raped young girls in a village in the municipality of Suva Reka (Shuareke). As was the case in Bosnia, gathering evidence that rape was widespread or systematic was important for establishing the culpability of superior officers for sexual assaults their subordinates committed. Under a statute of the Hague Tribunal, a commander can be prosecuted for rapes committed by his subordinates if he ordered or aided and abetted the rapes, or if he "knew or had reason to know that the subordinate was about to commit such acts" or had already done so and then failed to take "the necessary and reasonable measures to prevent such acts or to punish the perpetrators."

Late in the afternoon on April 17, a middle-aged man named Mustafa Gashi sought me out as I moved through the crowds of refugees at the border crossing. "Take it," he said, handing me a faded identification card. "It was my mother's. Take it as evidence to The Hague."

Retreating to a grassy knoll, now littered with plastic water bottles and paper refuse, we sat down and he told me his story. The day before, as Serb policemen swept through his neighborhood in Mitrovica, he hurried the eight members of his family into his green van and fled the city. "I was driving and my father, Muharrem, was in the passenger seat. We had passed through the village of Ljusta (Lushte) when I noticed a green civilian truck coming toward us in the opposite direction. It was moving slowly enough that I could make out two men in camouflage uniforms with white head scarves. Then I heard the sound

Serb police and militiamen often stopped tractor convoys at checkpoints to search for men and boys of fighting age. The young boy in the far right corner of the photograph disguised himself as a girl to escape detection.

of a gunshot. A single shot, like pop!…that was it. Everyone started screaming, and when I looked over my shoulder I saw my mother slumped over and blood soaking through her clothes."

Too frightened to stop, Mustafa kept driving while the women wrapped his mother in a blanket. When night fell he pulled off the road into a secluded spot and waited for the dawn. "That night was horrible. We argued and argued about what to do with my mother's body. It was too undignified to bury her there, in the middle of nowhere. And, anyway, we had no hand tools."

The next morning, as Mustafa and his family passed by the village of Velika Krusa (Krushe e Mahde), they noticed several mounds of fresh dirt in the village cemetery. Using their hands and pieces of cardboard, Mustafa and his father opened one of the graves. About a meter down, they uncovered a hand and then a forearm. "My father couldn't take it, and he started to cry. So, I told him to go back to the van. I quickly placed my mother in the grave, covered her with soil, and left."

Mustafa took me over to his van and introduced me to his family and showed me where the bullet had entered. I gave him my notebook and he drew a map of the graveyard with the arrangement of the graves along with the approximate location of his mother's grave. "Take The Hague there," he said, as he handed the notebook back. "They'll find all the evidence they'll ever need."

On May 24, 1999, the Hague Tribunal issued an indictment charging Slobodan Milosevic and four co-defendants "with crimes against humanity and violations of the laws of war for planning, instigating, ordering, committing or otherwise aiding and abetting in a campaign of terror and violence directed against the Kosovo Albanian civilians living in Kosovo of the Federal Republic of Yugoslavia." The core of the court's indictment was based on detailed accounts of massacres carried out by Serb forces in seven villages and towns throughout the province.

Most of the refugees living in camps in Macedonia and Albania first learned of the indictment in the pages of *Koha Ditore* (Daily Times). Once Kosovo's most widely read Albanian language newspaper, *Koha Ditore* was forced to close its editorial offices in Pristina on March 24, the day NATO bombing began. That day the police stormed the editorial offices and shot and killed a guard. As Serb forces rampaged through the city, most of the newspaper's staff went into hiding and then fled or were expelled from the country. Within weeks, they had re-assembled near the refugee camps in northwestern Macedonia and begun publishing their newspaper-in-exile. It became an important source of information for hundreds of thousands of Kosovar Albanians scattered in refugee camps throughout the region. It also was an uplifting sign that their society had not been completely destroyed.

Qamil Shehu, a 70-year-old refugee living in a camp near Kukes and a survivor of a massacre included in the Tribunal's indictment, took a special interest in the front page story in the *Koha Ditore*. Two months earlier, on the morning of March 26, a column of Serb tanks and several buses loaded with military policemen and paramilitaries had arrived at his village in southwestern Kosovo. Most of the residents of Mala Krusa (Krushe e Vogel) were ethnic Albanian, but Serbs lived there as well. Having caught wind of an army offensive, a handful of the town's Serb men donned militia uniforms and waited on the highway for the column's arrival. One of the men, Dragan Gavric, was a close friend of Qamil's. They had grown up together, and, until recently, worked side by side in the local winery. At approximately 5 a.m., the column stopped at the entrance to the village. A road block was hastily set up, and the Serbs began shelling the village. When the bombardment ended at mid-day, the militiamen descended on the village, rounding up 107 men and boys. The youngest were two of

Qamil's nephews, Xhelal and Mehmet Shehu, just 13. The oldest, at 72, was Bali Avdyli. Among them were a middle-aged man who suffered from cerebral palsy and a mentally retarded boy who was a month shy of his sixteenth birthday. As soldiers forced the women onto the highway, the militiamen marched the men into a hay barn and opened fire with their AK-47s. Miraculously, Shehu and three other men survived and managed to escape from the barn and flee to Albania.

In late June, two weeks after NATO tanks had rumbled into Kosovo, Qamil and his neighbors returned to Mala Krusa. They found it gutted, the houses burnt, the livestock slaughtered. The Serbs had fled. One night a group of children ran amok through the center of the village, burning and looting Serb homes. When they arrived at Dragan Gavric's house, they took special delight in pulling family portraits from the walls and hurling them into the street.

Many elderly refugees
collapsed from
exhaustion after they
passed through the gates
at the Morina crossing.

A man dragged his ailing grandmother across the border in a cart, probably used in a car repair shop.

A young woman waited for her family to arrive at the Morina crossing.

Two men huddled in blankets as
they paced back and forth at the
Morina crossing. Earlier that
morning, Yugoslav troops had
entered their village of Petrovo
Selo (Petrove) and forced the
men onto buses. They were told
that they would be digging
trenches near the Albanian
border, but when they arrived
there they were ordered off the
buses and told to walk to
Albania. Dozens of men from
Petrovo Selo waited day and
night at the Morina crossing for
their families to arrive.

An elderly woman took shelter from the wind and rain at the Morina crossing. Too frightened to travel further without her family, she slept on a piece of cardboard on the steps of the border station. Many elderly Kosovar Albanians became separated from their families as Serb forces swept through towns and cities in early morning raids.

Two men sought shelter from the rain as they waited for their families to arrive at the Morina crossing.

The mass exodus of ethnic Albanians from Kosovo in the spring of 1999 caught international relief organizations utterly unprepared.

Refugees gathered on a grassy knoll near the Morina crossing to rest before continuing their trek down the mountain valley to the refugee camps in Kukes. Many refugees had traveled night and day through Kosovo's forests and valleys in a desperate attempt to avoid Serbian forces.

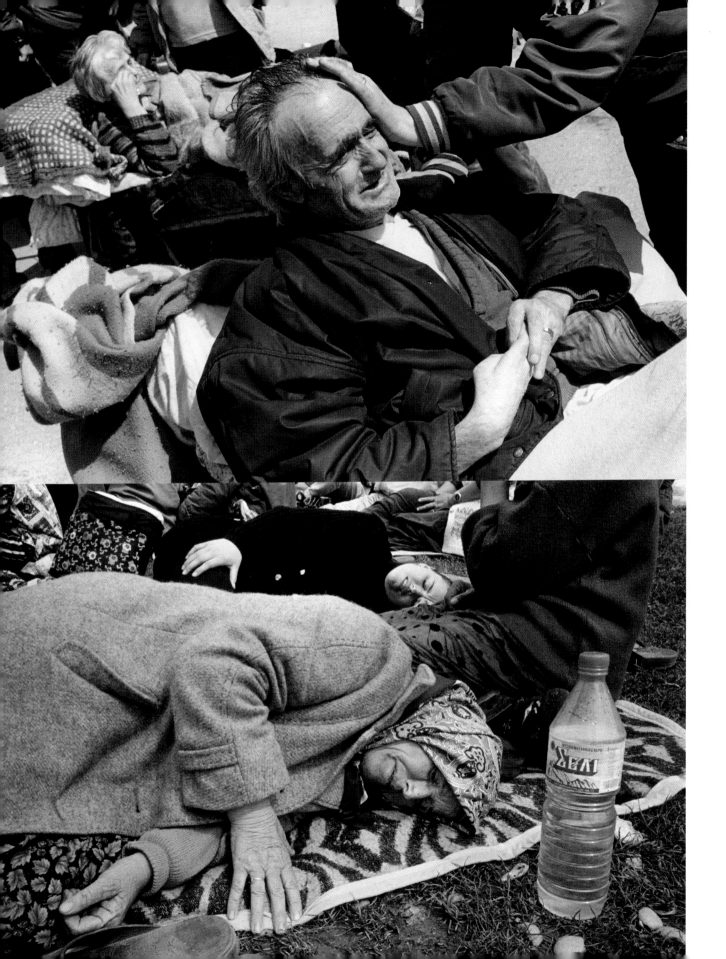

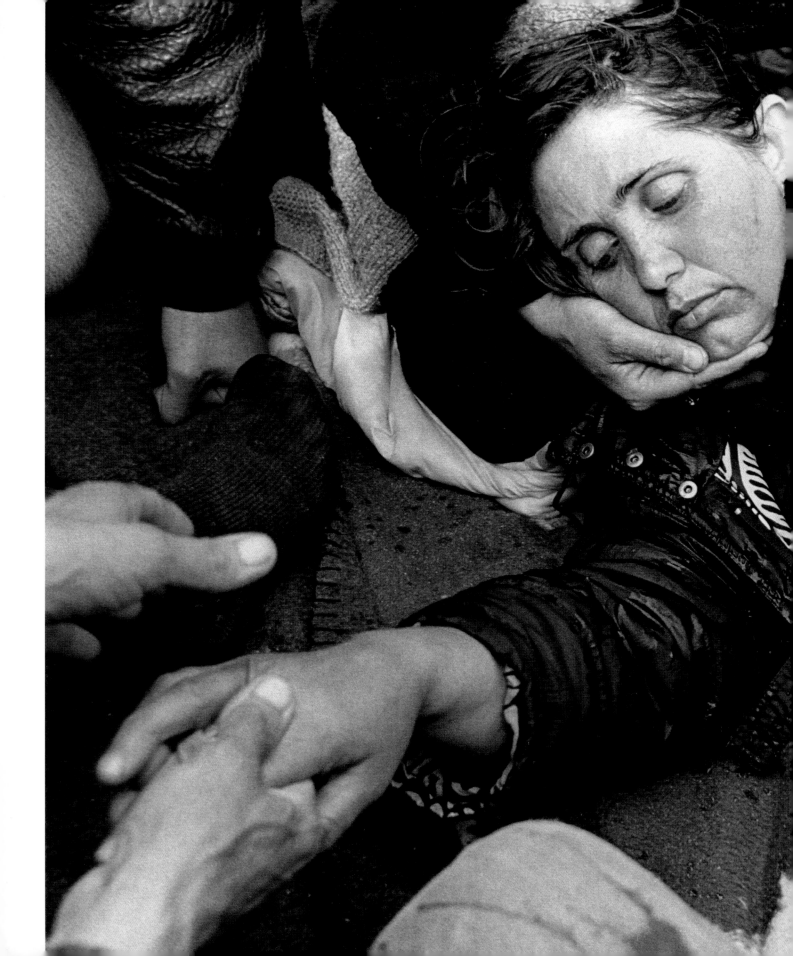

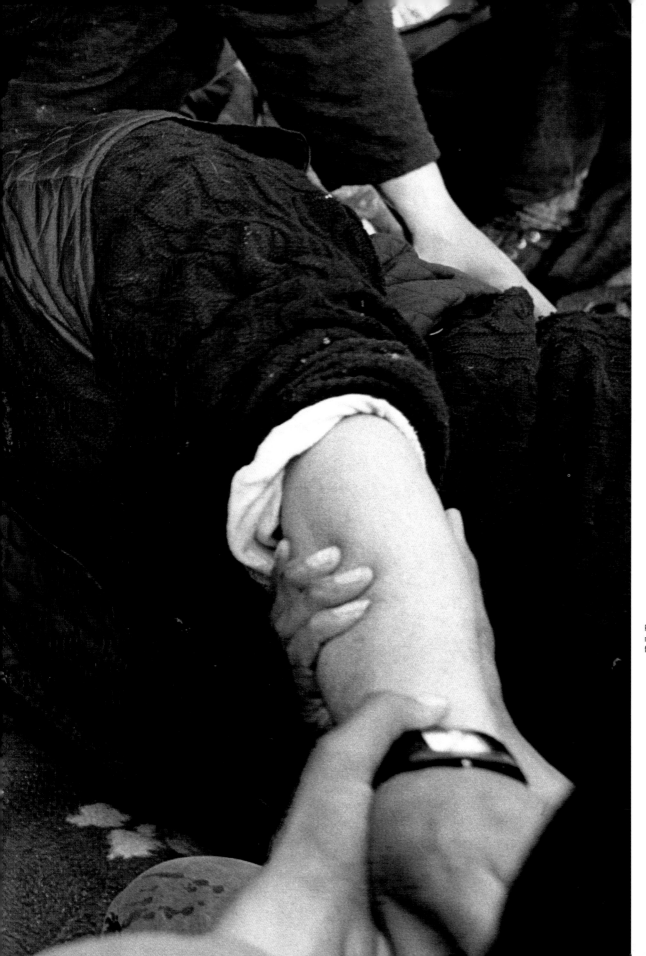

Refugees struggle to revive a woman who has fainted in her hay wagon.

Refugees left the Morina crossing and traveled 16 kilometers down a dirt road to refugee camps in Kukes.

One April evening we came upon a burial party along the road from Morina to Kukes. Several men stood in a circle looking on as other men used shovels to peel back the rocky earth. Their hay carts, led by stout horses, stood a few yards away beside a stand of poplars, and from underneath the plastic sheeting their women and children peered out.

Next to the grave was the body of an old woman, lying on a thick blanket. She was dressed in a white kerchief and flowing *shallvare* trousers, her hands and wrists swaddled in bloody bandages. No one knew her name nor where she was from.

She must have been well into her 80s. Earlier that day, the men had discovered her slumped in a ditch, delirious and begging for water, near a checkpoint on the other side of the border. Serb policemen had broken her wrists because her son was a KLA fighter, she said. She soon drifted into unconsciousness, and two kilometers beyond Morina, she died.

The men placed the body gently in the grave and covered it with earth. One of them said a prayer and they hoisted the shovels over their shoulders and walked slowly back to the road.

Refugees occupy an abandoned bus on the road to Kukes.

Following pages: Hundreds of thousands of Kosovar Albanians took refuge in camps in Kukes.

The most squalid camp in Kukes was on the grounds of an abandoned potato factory. Thousands of people lived in the factory's parking lot under makeshift tents constructed from scraps of wood and plastic sheeting.

NATO air strikes in Kosovo and Serbia killed and injured some 500 civilians. The young boy in the left of the photograph lost his parents when a NATO plane mistakenly bombed the tractor convoy he was traveling in outside of Djakovica (Gjakove).

Refugees in Kukes
scavenged for scraps of
wood for cooking fires.

Following pages:
Kukes's playing fields,
theaters, and parking lots
had been converted into
makeshift camps.

A few refugees were
housed with town
residents, but the vast
majority lived in tent
camps, which the spring
rains had turned into
muddy quagmires.

Young boys play a game of tag in the parking lot of an abandoned potato factory that had been turned into a camp for thousands of refugees.

We found Havere Shala in a room at the potato factory. She was a 90-year-old widow, who was blind and unable to walk long distances. Propped up on a folded blanket in a corner of the room, she listened intently to the commotion around her. That morning aid workers had announced that everyone staying in the factory would be bused to towns and villages in the interior of Albania. Families, on their way out the door, would stop by Havere's bedroll and wish her goodbye. By noon she was alone in the room.

Havare lived with her two sons in a village near Mitrovica. On April 15, 1999, as shells rained down on the village, Havere's two sons carried her down into the cellar. "I told them that it was better to leave me there than to carry me up into the hills," she said. The next day a neighbor loaded her onto his hay cart and brought her to Kukes.

"I can't leave," she said. "I have six daughters. Some of them must be looking for me. They're my only hope."

With nowhere else to go, refugees moved into the abandoned theater in downtown Kukes.

"It's not a safe place at all," one woman said. "There are town hooligans around here who prey on us at night. My husband and I have been robbed twice. He is a carpenter, and the last time they took his tool kit. What are we going to do now?"

With funding from the World Food Programme, local bakers produced over 6,000 loaves of bread a day to feed the refugees in Kukes. At dusk, a green truck would cruise through the camps, and aid workers would toss out loaves of bread and vegetables as children ran after the truck fighting for every scrap of food.

A young boy waited in a soup line at a refugee camp run by the Italian government.

In an effort to break the monotony of camp life in Kukes, UNICEF set up a makeshift school in the town theater and offered drawing and singing classes. However, many children in the camps feared leaving their mothers and grandparents and walking through the crowded, often chaotic streets to attend the school.

A man carried loaves of bread to
a refugee camp in Kukes.

Refugees often went to bed
hungry, though there was little
malnutrition in the camps. The
real enemies were dysentery,
respiratory infections, and the
nightmares brought on by terror
and loss.

Latrines stood in a
muddy field in a camp
operated by Médecins
sans Frontières.

Fresh graves appeared overnight in the Kukes cemetery. Death often claimed the most vulnerable: the sick, elderly, and newborns.

Men awaited the arrival of the newspaper *Koha Ditore* (Daily Times) in a refugee camp in Macedonia.

Once Kosovo's most widely read Albanian-language daily, *Koha Ditore* was forced to close its editorial offices in Pristina on March 24, the day NATO bombing began. The staff later re-grouped in northwestern Macedonia and began publishing their newspaper-in-exile. It soon became an important source of information for hundreds of thousands of Kosovar Albanians scattered in camps throughout the region.

Two ethnic Albanian men at a border crossing near Skopje, Macedonia described how they were tortured in a Serbian police station.

Torture was common in Kosovo before the war, but it increased dramatically after human rights monitors with the Organization for Security and Cooperation in Europe (OSCE) withdrew from the province just before the NATO air strikes. During the OSCE presence in Kosovo, reports of ill-treatment and torture were frequently the

subject of consultations with Serbian authorities and local police commanders.

During the NATO bombings, police powers in Kosovo were extended significantly by legislation proclaiming a state of war. According to the Yugoslav Federal Constitution the right to freedom from torture and ill-treatment cannot be derogated even during a state of war. Even so, Serbian forces, including notoriously brutal paramilitary units, used torture and beatings

as part of a coercive effort to make ethnic Albanians leave their homes or to hand over money.

Several refugees at the Morina border crossing told of beatings by the Serbian police and paramilitaries. "At one of the checkpoints two special policemen came up to our tractor trailer," 50-year-old Isuf Shala said as he tilted his head to the side to reveal a large purple welt. "They demanded all our money. I was the only grown man among us, and when I hesitated, one of

them hit me on the side of the head with his rifle butt and then shoved the gun barrel into my mouth. The women quickly handed over 500 DM, as well as all of their jewelry and even our bread and sugar."

A refugee waited for NATO troops to pass by on their way into Kosovo.

On June 9, 1999, NATO and Yugoslav commanders signed the Military Technical Agreement to stop the bombing and allow for the deployment of NATO troops in Kosovo. The following day, the UN Security Council adopted resolution 1244, which mandated a UN administration in the province.

Refugees began arriving in Macedonia in mid-March 1999, only to find that the Macedonian government and many Macedonian citizens did not want them there. Local officials confined this group for hours in extreme heat on a bus between the border and the Stenkovac refugee camp. Tens of thousands of other Kosovo refugees were accommodated or assisted by Macedonia's large ethnic Albanian population.

RETURN

On my way back to Kosovo that summer I stopped at the International Criminal Tribunal for the former Yugoslavia in The Hague to speak with Graham Blewitt, the Tribunal's deputy prosecutor. Located in a heavily guarded building along a tree-lined avenue, the Tribunal is a cold, secretive place, a sort of subdued hospital for the Balkan heart, staffed not only by judges but also by hundreds of prosecutors and investigators and translators and clerical workers and security guards.

Blewitt, a robust man in his early 50s, is a survivor. An Australian lawyer who once tracked down organized crime figures and suspected Nazi war criminals in New South Wales, he has served under three chief prosecutors since the Tribunal was established in 1993. "Kosovo," Blewitt told me, "was the turning point for the Tribunal. Kosovo marked a recognition on the part of NATO and the international community that the work of the Tribunal was a primary objective."

Supporters have viewed the court as a crucial tool for ending the cycle of violence and retribution individual political leaders have long manipulated in countries like Rwanda and the former Yugoslavia. By establishing individual guilt, the argument goes, the trials would help dispel the notion of collective blame for war crimes and acts of genocide. As Karl Jaspers said of the Nuremberg Trials in 1946, "For us Germans this trial has the advantage that it distinguishes between the particular crimes of the leaders and that it does not condemn the Germans collectively."

Such trials, supporters claim, can foster respect for democratic institutions by demonstrating that no individual—whether a foot soldier or high government official—is above the law. Insofar as legal proceedings confer legitimacy on otherwise contestable facts, trials also make it more difficult for individuals and societies to take refuge in denial. Some liberal legal theorists even view trials as a kind of moral pedagogy. They contend that tribunals, through their ability to distinguish between proper and improper conduct, can help postwar societies foster virtues of tolerance and reconciliation, forge a "shared truth" of past events, and reshape national identities.

Admirable goals. But governments, at least in the early years of the Tribunal's operation, failed to provide the court with adequate funding and intelligence information. Nor were they willing at first to risk the safety of their troops by removing mines and guarding suspected mass grave sites, let alone arresting suspected war criminals. "In Bosnia, we had to fight every step of the way to get support from the NATO forces," Blewitt said. "It eventually came, but it wasn't easy. In Kosovo it was very different. When the air strikes started we knew the day was going to come when we would be inside on the ground."

The bombing of Yugoslavia ended on June 10, 1999, and the Tribunal's investigators did indeed go rolling into Kosovo, with NATO's armed contingents. "As we went in," Blewitt said, "we already had several governments backing us, giving us forensic teams, and demining and securing crime scenes." The Tribunal's work had international priority and media exposure, as it had not in Croatia and Bosnia. What is more, the U.S. government had put a bounty of up to five million dollars each on the heads of the five co-defendants.

The indictments announced in The Hague on May 27 charged former Yugoslav president Slobodan Milosevic, Serb president Milan Milutinovic, former Deputy Prime Minister Nikola Sainovic, Chief of Staff Dragoljub Ojdanic, and former Serb Minister of Internal Affairs Vlajko Stojiljkovic with three counts each of crimes against humanity and one each of violation of the laws and customs of war. Of the two types of charges, violations of the laws and customs of war, or war crimes, is the older and more traditional.

"The mere fact that two armies or two parties are killing each other is not a war crime," Blewitt noted. "It is only when the parties step beyond the bounds of what is accepted. And modern-day armies are taught what constitutes the laws and customs of war." In essence, these laws define what are legal, illegal, and criminal acts in time of war. They acknowledge that death and suffering are inevitable in armed conflict, but that deliberately inflicting unnecessary suffering, especially upon civilians, constitutes a criminal act for which civilian and military leaders and their subordinates can be held accountable. If an army unit shells a tank column and happens to kill civilians, it has not necessarily committed a war crime, but if it deliberately targets hospitals, it has. Killing or torturing prisoners, civilians, or hostages is a war crime, as is burning crops and killing livestock to starve civilians or any other extensive destruction not justified by military necessity.

The most serious charge against the Serb and Yugoslav leaders was "crimes against humanity." The term originated in the Preamble to the 1907 Hague Convention, which codified the customary law of armed conflict. In 1915, the Allies accused the Ottoman Empire of crimes against humanity. Thirty years later, in 1945, the United States and other Allies incorporated it in the Nuremberg charter, which served as the *corpus juris* for levying charges against Nazi leaders following World War II. Crimes against humanity encompass a wide range of abominable acts—mass murder, extermination, enslavement, deportation—committed against civilians on a large scale. The accounts of rapes, murders, and mass expulsions that Fred Abrahams and I and other investigators had heard along Kosovo's borders in the spring of 1999 and later verified in the towns and villages throughout Kosovo clearly met this definition. The charge of crimes against humanity also places an onus on all governments to arrest anyone indicted for such a crime. In effect, a person who commits crimes against humanity is, like the pirate or slave trader before him, *hostis humani generis*, an enemy of all humankind—over whom any state could hold criminal jurisdiction.

If Slobodan Milosevic and his co-defendants faced serious charges, punishable with life imprisonment, for their actions in Kosovo, Graham Blewitt and his investigators also had some serious investigative work ahead of them. In effect, they had to prove, beyond a shadow of a doubt, that the crimes committed by Yugoslav forces against civilians in villages like Cuska and Mala Krusa were not just an accident but had been planned and were widespread and systematic. "In the absence of direct evidence of a plan to massacre these people," Blewitt explained, "we have to rely on circumstantial evidence. So proving patterns is important. We have to demonstrate that the tactics used by Yugoslav military, police, and paramilitary units in, say, village A were the same as those in village B on or about the same day and thereafter in village C and village D. We don't have to prove every single murder, or every single massacre, we just need to select a sample of these so that we can prove a pattern of killing and destruction aimed against civilians."

In building their case of crimes against humanity, the prosecution will need to go back to the late 1980s when the Serbs began targeting Kosovar Albanians by removing them from all public employment. It started with the dismissal of ethnic Albanian doctors, lawyers, and public officials, Blewitt noted. "And then you add to that the fact that rapes and assaults and beatings and torturings

NATO tanks rumbled into Kosovo on June 11, 1999. As the Yugoslav Army and Serbian police units withdrew, crowds of ethnic Albanians jammed the streets of Pristina (Prishtina) and other cities and towns, cheering the European and American soldiers as if they were liberators.

But, in reality, NATO's war had been fought entirely from 15,000 feet in the air, and none of these young "conquering heroes," sidelined in Macedonia and Albania during the fighting, had seen a day of combat. They were entering Kosovo to keep the peace but would soon discover the reality of the ancient proverb: *amat victoria curam* (Victory loves trouble).

Crowds cheered a NATO tank as it entered Pristina, the capital of Kosovo.

Kosovar Albanians danced in the streets as NATO troops entered the town of Prizren.

British paratroopers with the NATO-lead Kosovo Force (KFOR) received flowers from well-wishers along a highway.

KFOR would soon learn that rebuilding a war-ravaged society required time, persistence, tolerance, accountability, and money. All of which, it seemed, were in short supply in postwar Kosovo. Despite their repeated promises, the same governments that had fought the war to drive the Serbs out of the province—and basked in its glory—were reluctant to finance the day-to-day operations of the United Nations authority they had installed until local governance could be re-established. "Running Kosovo is hard enough without running around the world with a begging bowl," the director of the UN protectorate in Kosovo, Bernard Kouchner, told the *New York Times* in March 2000.

With only one-quarter the authorized personnel and one-tenth the necessary money, Kouchner and his staff struggled to create a new civil administration and judicial system for the province as well as provide such basic services as health care, sanitation, and road repair. Meanwhile, on Kosovo's streets and back roads, NATO troops and police were grappling, with little success, to stay the hand of vengeance raised by mostly young Kosovar Albanians seeking to settle scores with their former Serbian and Roma neighbors. NATO was unwilling, for political and security reasons, to confront the Kosovo Liberation Army, which was linked to much of the violence, as well as growing criminality in Kosovo.

British KFOR troops
arrested men suspected
of belonging to the
Kosovo Liberation Army.
With a nonfunctioning
judiciary, many suspects
were held briefly and
released.

KLA fighters let off a
volley of shots to
honor the burial of a
group of villagers
killed during the war.

Unable to identify all of the victims, many villages have had to bury their dead in communal graves.

pointed to the list of men reportedly killed in Mala Krusa on March 26, 1999. There were 103 names. Thirty-five of them had the last name of Shehu.

Qamil took the document and ran his finger slowly along the edge of the page. Speaking in a low voice, he read the names out loud: "Destan, that is my brother... Dritan, my cousin... Mentor, another cousin." He stopped at the name of "Qamil Shehu" and smiled slightly, "So they think I'm dead." He continued down the list: "Haziz, he is my younger brother... Myftar, also my brother." When he reached the last two names, his face hardened and he pressed his finger firmly against the page. "Samit and Veli Shehu," he said, "they are my sons."

A gust of wind sent ashes and dust swirling about our feet.

"Could you imagine ever living again with Gavric and the other Serbs in the village?" I asked. He thought for a minute, shifting his feet and looking from the charred remains of the house to the darkening sky. "Before, we were neighbors," he said in a voice thick with anger. "We went to each others' weddings. We worked together and drank together. Before all this, we never had anything bad with them. But today, I could eat them with my teeth."

As Qamil spoke, I could feel him slipping into what writer Michael Ignatieff has called "the dream-time of vengeance." Many of us who wrote about the wars in Bosnia and Croatia found that as we listened to atrocity stories it was occasionally difficult to determine, as Ignatieff writes, "whether these stories had occurred yesterday or in 1941 or 1841 or 1441. For the tellers of the tale, yesterday and today were the same." The dreamtime of vengeance, he writes, is a somniferous, timeless state, where time past and time present are indistinguishable, "a place where crimes can never be safely fixed in the past, but remain locked in the eternal present."

"How can I ever forgive what happened?" Qamil asked me, his voice swelling with anger. "I can't even bury the bodies of my brothers and sons. No, now I only have hate."

"The revenge fantasy," writes psychiatrist Judith Herman, "is often a mirror image of the traumatic memory, in which the roles of perpetrator and victims are reversed. It often has the same grotesque, frozen, and wordless quality as the traumatic memory itself." In his humiliated fury, Qamil imagines that revenge is the only way to rid himself of the shame and restore his own sense of power. This is the only way to force the perpetrator to truly acknowledge the harm done to him, he feels.

Survivors must come to terms with the impossibility of getting even or they'll remain forever imprisoned in the dreamtime of vengeance, Herman and other mental health specialists argue. "Pain," writes Donald W. Schriver, Jr., "can shear the human memory in two crippling ways: with forgetfulness of the past or imprisonment in it. The mind that insulates the traumatic past from conscious memory plants a bomb in the depths of the psyche—it takes no great grasp of psychiatry to know that. But the mind that fixes on pain risks getting trapped in it. Too horrible to remember, too horrible to forget."

Giving up the fantasy of revenge does not mean giving up the quest for justice; on the contrary, a quest truly begins with the process of joining with others to hold the perpetrator accountable for his crimes. But accepting the rule of law comes with a price: victims must abandon any desire to physically harm the person who has wronged them and, so it is hoped, break the cycle of vengeance. If Milosevic were ever brought to trial, Qamil would eagerly testify for the prosecution, he told me.

92

But, he added, it was more important personally for him to see that Dragan Gavric pay for his crime—a wish, given the Tribunal's strategy of targeting only the big fish, that will probably never be realized.

Qamil is hardly alone in his desire for retribution. Since NATO troops entered Kosovo in June 1999, Kosovar Albanians have driven thousands of Serbs out of the province or into enclaves and murdered dozens of others in cold blood. In its 1999 report, *Kosovo/Kosova: As Seen, As Told*, the Organization for Security and Cooperation in Europe describes hundreds of incidents where ethnic Albanians have attacked and looted Serb homes. On March 16, 2001, in perhaps the worst incident so far, suspected KLA members set off a bomb on the Serbian side of the border, killing 11 Serbian civilians. The International Committee of the Red Cross places the number of Serbs missing after the withdrawal of Serbian troops in June 1999 at 542, but Serbian activists argue that the correct figure is over 1,000.

Younger generations of Albanians, who have known Serbs only as oppressors, have shown a growing intolerance of all ethnic others, including Roma and Muslim Slavs. People under the age of 30 now make up more than half the population and many young Kosovars manifest a thirst for blind revenge that sickens their parents, many of whom still have personal memories of peaceful coexistence with the Serbs. Gangs of youth, between the ages of 12 and 20, have harassed, beaten, and threatened defenseless victims, especially elderly Serbs.

Unlike Qamil's wishes for revenge, which are targeted at a few individuals, the type of vengeance that has taken hold of Kosovo's youth is blind and arbitrary and often directed at the innocent. One horrific incident took place in the evening of November 29, 1999, when a mob of ethnic Albanians dragged a Serb man and two Serb women from their car in downtown Pristina, beat all three, and fatally shot the man. The murder victim was 62-year-old Dragoslav Basic, a university professor specializing in earthquake engineering, a discipline he had learned at the University of California, Berkeley, on a Fullbright Scholarship in the late 1980s. Dragoslav Basic had returned to Kosovo in 1990 to teach at the University of Kosovo. The other victims were his 51-year-old wife, Dragica Basic, and his 71-year-old mother-in-law, Borka Jovanovic. Both women suffered critical injuries, including extensive lesions to the face caused when their attackers struck them and jammed firecrackers into their mouths. Borka Jovanovic was so badly beaten she hemorrhaged into her lungs and her spleen had to be removed.

"I cannot hide my shame to discover that, for the first time in our history, we, Kosovo Albanians, are also capable of monstrous acts," wrote the internationally respected publisher Veton Surroi in late 1999. "I have to speak out to make it clear that our moral code, by which women, children and elderly should be left unharmed, has been and is being violated."

Throughout Kosovo, the real and perceived role of ordinary Serbs in crimes against humanity has proven cancerous, especially among the young. This is compounded by the fact that the killings especially in the villages were so intimate. In Bosnia men were often rounded up and trucked away to be executed, while in Kosovo children watched as paramilitaries, some of whom were their Serb neighbors, backed by Serbian police and Yugoslav soldiers, murdered family members and burned their homes. "I fear for the children a lot," Mary Ellen Keough told me in her office in Pristina. A 52-year-old community health specialist from Massachusetts, Keough was the director of family support services for Physicians for Human Rights in Kosovo. "The children have witnessed so much here. Obviously, they are at a young, impressionable age and have developed firm memories of what they've seen. They are disturbed. You can see it in their faces. Parents have told me that their children are misbehaving more now than before the war. They are harder to discipline. They also have trouble sleeping... I think you'll need a couple of generations removed from this kind of viewing of atrocities... for the emotional rebuilding of Kosovo to take place."

Qamil Shehu, like many Kosovar Albanians, wants justice, but doesn't believe the small fry like Dragan Gavric will ever be captured and brought to trial. Many of the killers fled in June to Serbia or Montenegro, where they now live without fear of arrest or reprisals. Since no court has indicted them, they are free to travel throughout the region, or even emigrate to the very countries which once bombed them. Moreover, the prospects are slim that the Tribunal will ever reach down through the ranks and indict many of the garden variety killers.

What role will the Tribunal play in the process of rebuilding Kosovo? Will trials help stay the hand of vengeance?

To begin with, indicting Milosevic has been an important first step. Albanian Kosovars, Bosnian Muslims, Croats, and many Serbs celebrated the announcement of his indictment. After the war anti-Milosevic protesters in Belgrade could be heard chanting a new admonition: "To The Hague, to The Hague, Slobodan to The Hague." The laborious process of collecting testimonies and establishing the facts— Who killed whom? Where were the bodies buried? Who were the killers? Did the bullet enter from behind or from the front? And at what range?— may one day pay off by putting Milosevic and his henchmen behind bars. Factual evidence also can help shield the truth from the slings and arrows of future revisionists and make it difficult for individuals and societies to take refuge in denial. As forensic anthropologist Clyde Snow has said: "It's awfully hard to argue with a single gunshot wound to the head."

The presence of foreign journalists, forensic investigators, and researchers from organizations like Human Rights Watch both on the border and, later, in the destroyed villages of Kosovo had a subtle, and perhaps unintended, effect on Kosovars. As researcher Fred Abrahams learned in Cuska, villagers did not see him as merely an investigator gathering information for a report, but as a bearer of a more intangible message: recognition and acknowledgment of all that they had suffered. By identifying victims and determining the cause of death, forensic investigators like Kevin Berry were also helping the survivors of the assault on their village to free themselves from the limbo of despair. Caught between hope and grief, many of these survivors longed to know the fate of their loved ones. It consumed them night and day. And until they knew the truth, they would never be able to grieve properly.

Liberal law theorists and human rights activists argue that justice, like the pursuit of rights, is a universal, a historic practice that exists above politics. The Hague Tribunal, in its 1994 annual report, argued that it was essential to peace and security in the former Yugoslavia: "[I]t would be wrong to assume that the Tribunal is based on the old maxim *fiat justitia et pereat mundus* (let justice be done, even if the world were to perish). The Tribunal is, rather, based on the maxim propounded by Hegel in 1821: *fiat justitia ne pereat mundus* (let justice be done lest the world should perish." But such positivist notions fail to recognize that courts, like all institutions, exist because of, not in spite of, politics. People and entire communities can interpret a tribunal's decisions, procedures (modes and manner of investigation, selection of cases, timing of trials, types and severity of punishments), and even its very existence in a variety of ways. Indeed, politics in this sense is imbedded in everything, especially the pursuit of justice.

No one knew that better than Kevin Berry, who had to confront an angry group of villagers demanding that he stay and finish what he had begun. Faced with a clash that pitted the international needs of the Tribunal against the local needs of the villagers, he opted (wisely) not to move immediately to the next village but to remain in Mala Krusa and finish all of the exhumations. "They're right," he told me after the incident. "The Tribunal has to respect their wishes. They're waiting to see if their loved ones have been recovered… To leave now would be disrespectful."

War crime investigations and trials alone cannot address the root causes of communal violence, especially in a postwar country like Yugoslavia where thousands of people—strangers and neighbors alike—planned and carried out ethnic cleansing with impunity and terrible savagery. The logic of law, as Hannah Arendt suggests, can never make sense of the logic of atrocity, nor how it is interpreted by the survivors and perpetrators. Strictly legal interpretations of Kosovo's nightmare will always be skewed in the eyes of those accused of creating it: while trials of Milosevic and his co-defendants in The Hague may help Kosovar Albanians and their communities feel some small measure of vindication, the communities from which the Serb perpetrators came may feel as if they have been made scapegoats, especially if those local Serbs who participated in the killings and expulsions—the little fish—are never brought to justice. This is why factual truth doesn't always lead to reconciliation, nor should it necessarily be the Tribunal's objective in the Balkans.

Trials may help the rehabilitation of a defeated country, but only as one small element in a broader program of national reconstruction. The Tribunal at least can help to establish a definitive record of what took place and thus pierce the veil of denial and impunity held up by those who planned and carried out atrocities. At the same time, through its investigations and trials it can provide acknowledgment and recognition to the victims. These are important functions. To expect more of the Tribunal—or any tribunal—is wishful thinking.

Nasser Mazreku emerged from 78 days in hiding to meet a group of journalists on the Prizren-Djakovica road. They showed him the Hague Tribunal's indictment of Slobodan Milosevic and his co-defendants, which listed several massacre sites and the names of victims killed there. Upon finding the names of several of his family members who he thought had escaped to Albania, he broke down and cried.

KFOR troops and journalists found a brutal swath of death and destruction along the highway connecting the towns of Pec (Peja), Djakovica, and Prizren.

In the weeks following the initial NATO raids on Pristina and Belgrade in mid-March, Yugoslav and Serbian police and paramilitary forces had gone on a rampage in western Kosovo in an effort to rid the border region of all ethnic Albanians. Clearing the borderlands would minimize infiltration by KLA fighters from their bases in Albania. Milosevic also had an old score to settle with the ethnic Albanians in the western borderlands. Many of the villages along this stretch of road were known for their support of the KLA. Since 1998, arms had been flowing through these villages, and KLA fighters frequented the area, sometimes ambushing police on the main road. Some of the province's most fertile land is located in western Kosovo, which had caught the eye of paramilitaries particularly interested in war booty.

Under international law, destruction of property is permitted under certain circumstances. Article 52 of the 1977 Additional Protocol I to the Geneva Conventions allows attacks on "those objects which by their nature, location, purpose or use make an effective contribution to military action and whose total or partial destruction, capture or neutralization, in the circumstances ruling at the time, offers a definite military advantage." This provision addresses the situation of military forces making a direct attack on civilian objects and property for the purpose of destroying it. In the view of the villagers along the highway from Pec to Prizren, the deliberate and widespread destruction of their homes, businesses, places of worship, and farmlands served absolutely no concrete military purpose. Apparently, the prosecutors at the Hague Tribunal agreed as the killing and destruction along the Pec-Prizren corridor figures prominently in the Tribunal's indictment of Slobodan Milosevic and his four co-defendants.

A destroyed mosque, its rooms gutted and relics smashed, stands next to the road to Djakovica.

Yugoslav and Serbian troops deliberately shelled or otherwise damaged over a hundred mosques in Kosovo between March and June 1999. After the war, Kosovar Albanians damaged or destroyed dozens of Serbian Orthodox churches throughout the province.

Upon returning to Kosovo, ethnic Albanian refugees often found that the towns and villages they had left behind had been vandalized beyond recognition.

According to the OSCE, in the period of the escalation of the armed conflict from March 20 onwards, "deliberate destruction of civilian property, looting, and pillage were defining characteristics of the Yugoslav and Serbian forces. These attacks appeared to have a three-fold purpose: they were meant to weaken and undermine the Kosovar Albanian population, to serve as an additional profit incentive for the military and security forces and their collaborators, and to destroy houses to ensure that the population did not return after expulsion."

Although the practice of pillage in conflict has been prohibited for nearly a century, few countries and cultures are exempt from the charge. The 1907 Hague Convention states: "The pillage of a town or place, even when taken by assault is prohibited." Pillage and destruction of property are prohibited under Protocol II of the Geneva Conventions of 1949. These prohibitions are general in scope, and concern not only organized pillage but also pillage through individual acts without the consent of the military authorities. The Federal Republic of Yugoslavia, as a High Contracting Party to Protocol II, is obliged not only to stop but also to prevent all forms of pillaging.

A couple passed through the center of Djakovica on their horse-drawn cart after the Serbian withdrawal in June 1999. Government security forces had burned the city's old town on March 24 and 25.

Following pages:
The Serbian police headquarters in Pristina allegedly served as both a torture center and a clubhouse for torturers. Top: Wire garrotes; police caps and cards; a chair used for interrogations; and the police chief's desk. Middle: Bats and blades in an interrogation cell; brass knuckles; cap and evidence book; and pictures on the wall of a policeman's private quarters. *Bottom:* Located in the basement, license plates taken from Kosovar Albanians; hastily burned documents; police mug shots taken at the time of arrest or interrogation; a chain saw and various alleged torture instruments.

During the war many rural women lost their husbands and several male members of their family. As we learned in Bosnia, life could be very hard for these women, especially in rural communities where gender roles are so specific and where men tend to take on most interactions with the outside world.

Returning refugees
testified that this was the
site of a massacre near
the city of Djakovica.

An ethnic Albanian man collected bones and scraps of clothing of his relatives for burial in a village cemetery near Pec. Among the dead were 13 boys and 9 girls, all members of the Krasniqi family. Serb paramilitaries allegedly executed many members of the Krasniqi clan when they took control of the village in early May 1999. The oldest child was 19 years old.

"Kosovo is one vast crime scene," Louise Arbour, then Chief Prosecutor of the International Criminal Tribunal for the former Yugoslavia (ICTY), frequently told reporters as she toured massacre sites throughout the province in July 1999. Since the arrival of NATO troops a month earlier, Tribunal investigators had discovered a pattern in the terror that raced through the towns and villages of Kosovo earlier that spring. Serb police and paramilitaries would herd groups of civilians into homes or courtyards and open fire with automatic weapons. The bodies of the victims would then be set on fire in an effort to destroy the physical evidence.

As of July 2001, Tribunal investigators had recovered the remains of just over 4,300 people, of which approximately half had been positively identified. The vast majority, if not all, of the dead are believed to be ethnic Albanians, although it is possible that some of the remains belong to other ethnic groups. Approximately 3,000 ethnic Albanians remain missing in Kosovo.

"It is not really a numbers game to determine whether crimes against humanity have been committed," the Tribunal's deputy prosecutor Graham Blewitt said in an interview in July 1999. The number of dead in Kosovo is not as legally significant to the Tribunal's prosecutors and judges as is motive and method. Nor are numbers important to the families of the missing—Albanian and Serb alike—who want to know the fate of their loved ones and to bury their remains in a proper manner.

Without bodies and funerals, some relatives of the missing can not visualize the death of family members and thus accept it as real. They are caught in a limbo between hope and grief. Until they receive the remains of their loved ones, they can neither return to their past lives nor plan for the future.

Many homes were
destroyed by
indiscriminate artillery or
mortar fire.

Serb paramilitaries often rounded up groups of villagers and forced them into a house. They would then toss a grenade inside and set the house on fire.

In the village of Velika Krusa, a family photograph album, caked in mud, was found in late June 1999 amid a pile of luggage and clothing that had belonged to displaced Kosovar Albanians. The village is mentioned in the Hague Tribunal's indictment of Milosevic and his four co-defendants.

Following pages:
Rubble and wind now defined what was once a vibrant ethnic Albanian village near Djakovica.

The rotting corpse of a
dog marked a mass
grave near Djakovica in
western Kosovo.

Previous pages:

Wars often result in a variety of mass graves. Victorious troops may collect enemy dead and, though a violation of the laws of war, dump them in mass graves. Before fleeing combat zones, noncombatants may bury the victims of artillery attacks or bombing raids in common graves. Or, as was often the case in Kosovo, security forces can deliberately kill civilians and bury them in mass graves in an effort to hide their crimes.

Mass graves themselves can be a violation of international law. The Third and Fourth Geneva Conventions and Additional Protocol I contain provisions governing the proper burial, identification, and registration of those killed in war. Prisoners of war, for example, must be "honorably buried" in graves that bear information about them.

Tribunal investigators in Kosovo have experienced several false starts in their investigation of mass graves. Some graves were systematically emptied by Serb troops and special police units. At Izbica (Izbice), villagers told investigators that they had buried 143 bodies after a massacre carried out by Serb police and special forces in early April 1999. Spy satellite images taken by NATO, published in the international press two months later, showed 143 graves in nearly perfect rows spanning the breadth of an open field. But, in late June, when Tribunal investigators reached the village, the bodies had been removed and earthmovers had been used in a crude and unsuccessful attempt to erase the traces of the site. The same happened in Pusto Selo (Pastasel), near Orahovac, and the hamlet of Rezala (Rezalle), north of Pristina. Similarly, at Ljubenic (Lubeniq), near the western city of Pec, a widely publicized gravesite said to hold 350 bodies only held five.

In November 2000, Serb army and police sources told journalists Michael Montgomery and Stephen Smith of American RadioWorks that Milosevic's senior generals had ordered secret police units to remove and destroy corpses from massacre sites like Izbica. A member of one unit told the reporters that he was ordered to collect bodies from mass graves and truck them to the Trepca lead refinery, just outside of the city of Mitrovica. "I was told that [the blast furnace] was enough heat to destroy everything, every trace of the stuff they call DNA," he said. However, an investigation of the Trepca mine has so far turned up no evidence of any crime.

Meanwhile, contested facts and conflicting claims of culpability surround one of the massacre sites listed in the Tribunal's

indictment of Slobodan Milosevic and his four co-defendants. The incident involves an alleged mass execution of 45 people near the village of Racak (Recak), 32 kilometers southwest of Pristina, on January 15, 1999. The massacre reportedly took place seven days after a KLA attack against three police vehicles which left three policemen dead. Villagers claim that policemen and men in black uniforms and ski masks entered Racak early on the morning of January 15 and detained several men and executed them on a ridge near the village.
The following day, after visiting the massacre site, William Walker, then head of Kosovo mission of the Organization for Security and

Cooperation in Europe, declared in a press conference that "from what I saw, I do not hesitate to describe the event as a massacre, a crime against humanity. Nor do I hesitate to accuse the government security forces of responsibility."

Meanwhile, after conducting its own medicolegal investigation of the bodies with the participation of Finnish pathologists, the Yugoslav authorities informed the media that no grounds exist for bringing charges against Serbian police regarding the Racak incident. In January 2001, Yugoslav president Vojislav Kostunica said the killings at Racak were staged to look like a massacre to embarrass Yugoslavia.

These pages:
Foreign journalists discovered four bodies by the road near Zrze (Xerxe), Kosovo in mid-June 1999. The corpses appeared to be, at most, a week old. One of the victims had his hands tied together and his socks stuffed in his shoes. They were either the last victims of the Serbs or among the first victims of retribution by the Kosovo Liberation Army.

Since NATO troops entered Kosovo in June 1999, revenge has spread like an infectious disease among many Kosovar Albanian communities. Tens of thousands of ethnic Serbs and Romas have been driven out of the province or into enclaves, while dozens of others

have been murdered in cold blood. Returning refugees, many of whom lost their own property through theft and arson, have been particularly implicated in the expulsion of Serb and Roma from their homes. However, the most serious incidents of violence have been carried out by former members of the KLA.

Kosovar villagers
near Prizren reburied
a neighbor killed by
Serb forces.

THE CASE

TEXT BY
FRED ABRAHAMS
PHOTOGRAPHERS
UNKNOWN

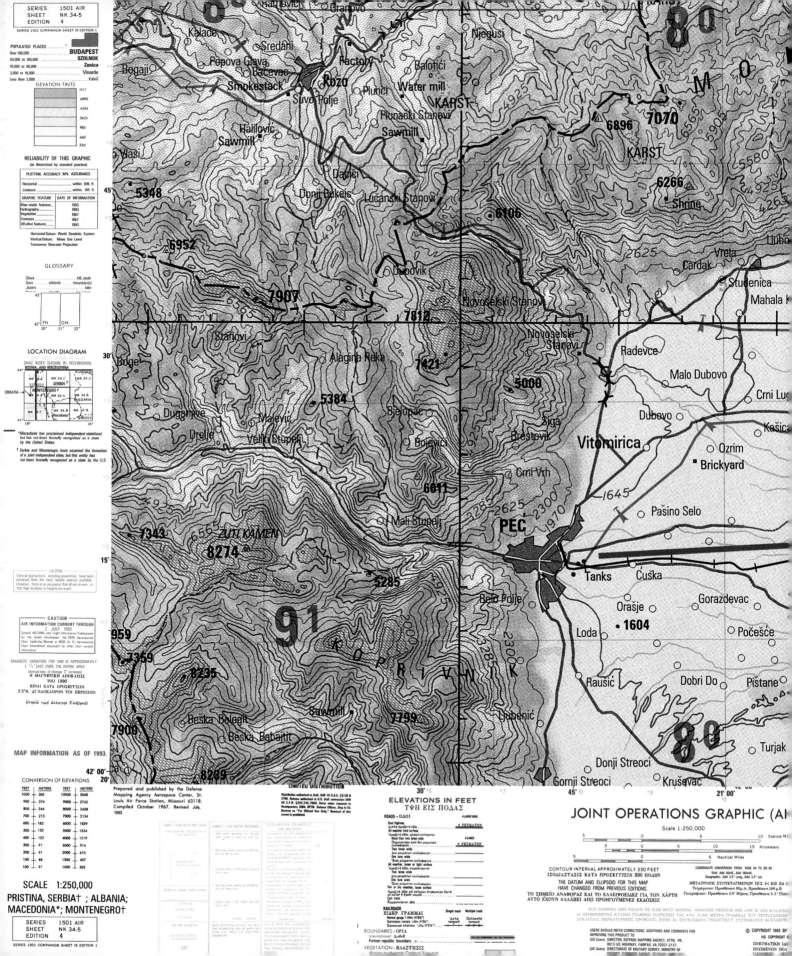

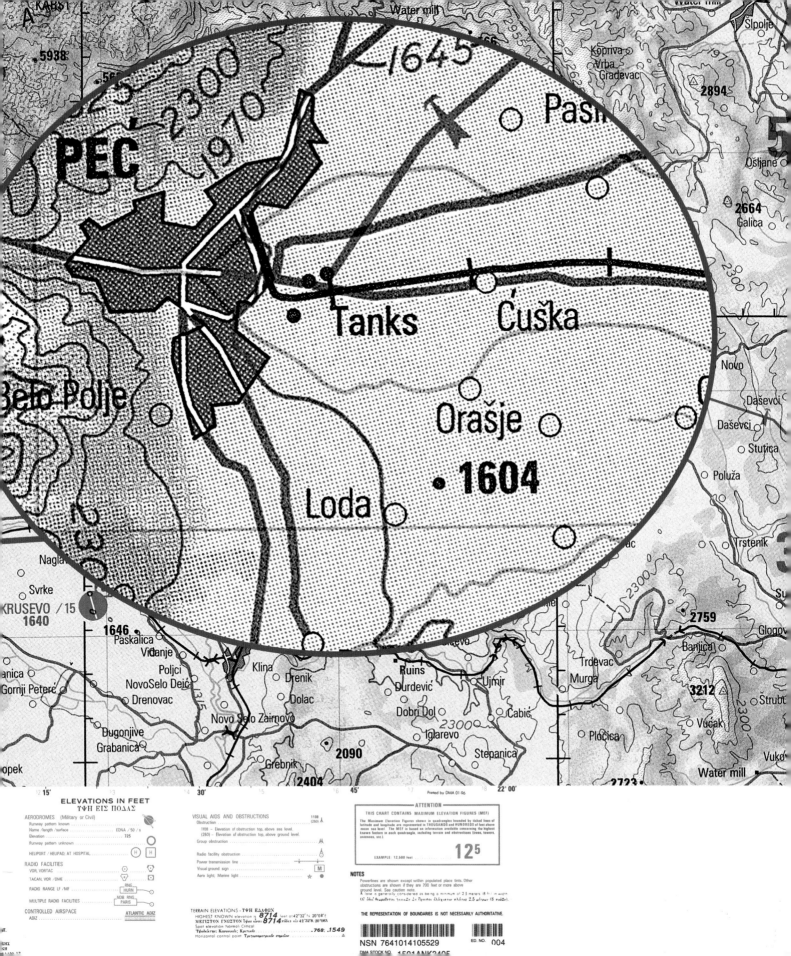

SUMMARY

This chapter documents what happened in one village on one day.

In the early morning of May 14, 1999, in the midst of NATO's air campaign against Yugoslavia, Serbian security forces descended on the small village of Cuska (Qyshk) near the western Kosovo city of Pec (Peje). Fearing reprisals, many men fled into the nearby hills while the rest of the population was forcibly assembled in the village center. Twelve men were killed in various parts of the village during the initial roundup.

At approximately 8:30 a.m., the security forces in green military uniforms with painted faces and masks separated the gathered women, children, and elderly from the remaining men who had not managed to flee. The more than 200 villagers were threatened and systematically robbed of their money, jewelry, and other valuables. Their identification papers were destroyed.

Thirty-two men between the ages of 19 and 69 were divided into three groups and taken into three separate houses, where they were forced to stand in a line. In each house, uniformed men sprayed them repeatedly with automatic weapons. In one of the houses, a gunman finished off several of the fallen men with pistol shots. Each house was set on fire and left to burn.

The events in Cuska are far from unique: thousands of ethnic Albanians were killed by Serbian special forces and paramilitaries throughout Kosovo between March and June 1999—many of them in a similar manner.

But this case has two special characteristics that make it worth a detailed investigation. First, in each of the three groups of men, there was one survivor. Through pure chance, three people managed to crawl from the burning homes, none of them seriously injured. They, and many others present that day, have told Human Rights Watch their stories.

Second, while ethnic Albanian villagers in Kosovo are usually unable to differentiate between soldiers, special police, and paramilitaries, let alone identify individuals, in this case there is powerful evidence to point the finger at some of the specific people involved in these war crimes. Local villagers are adamant that ethnic Serbs from the immediate area were involved in the action. Some of the forces spoke to the Albanians by name and asked for specific valuables.

More importantly, villagers positively identified in photographs two of the individuals that they claim were present in Cuska on May 14 and a third who was present in the nearby village of Zahac (Zahaq) on the same day, when nineteen other men were killed. While none of the individuals identified are known to have opened fire on the ethnic Albanian men, their presence in Cuska and Zahac on May 14 means that they should be able to identify the perpetrators, as well as the commanders of the unit. That information is invaluable to the International Criminal Tribunal for the former Yugoslavia, which is mandated to investigate and prosecute war crimes in Kosovo, as well as to local Yugoslav courts, which may begin some prosecutions after the October 2000 fall of Slobodan Milosevic. The photographs used to identify the men in Cuska were provided to Human Rights Watch by representatives of the Kosovo Liberation Army (KLA). While Human Rights Watch cannot vouch for the authenticity of the photographs, numerous Kosovar Albanians recognized the men mentioned in this report from these photographs, and placed them among the Serbian forces in the villages on the day of the killings. Some witnesses were able to provide names.

A Human Rights Watch researcher scanned the photographs into a laptop computer and then showed them to villagers in Cuska, Zahac, and Pavljan (Pavlan; ten people were killed in this village on May 14), as well as to people in Pec. The methodology employed was to show the photographs to only one person at a time, preferably in a one-on-one setting. All of the photographs were shown one at a time on the computer screen without any comment or suggestive hints.

Human Rights Watch found five different people, interviewed separately, who said the man second from the left in Exhibit Photo 1 was among the Serbian forces in Cuska on May 14. Three of these people thought the man was a commander. United States journalists independently investigating war crimes around Pec with the same photographs found three people who independently identified the man as Srecko Popovic. The journalists also found an additional five people who said they saw Popovic in Cuska on May 14.

Two of the witnesses Human Rights Watch spoke to claimed that the man in Exhibit Photos 2 (on right) and 3 had been in Cuska with the Serbian security forces. The man in both photographs appears to be the same as the man identified in Photo 1 as Srecko Popovic.

Three other people said that Zvonimir (Zvonko) Cvetkovic was also present in Cuska on May 14, one interviewed by Human Rights Watch and two by the U.S. journalists (Exhibit Photo 4, far right). The person who spoke with Human Rights Watch picked Cvetkovic out from the group photograph and said she saw him in Cuska on May 14. "Of course I know Zvonko," the witness said. "We lived on the same street." Human Rights Watch subsequently obtained a copy of Cvetkovic's passport (see Exhibit Photo 5).

Two ethnic Albanian men from Zahac, interviewed separately, identified Slavisa Kastratovic from Exhibit Photo 1 (third from left), and said that they had seen him in Zahac on May 14. Both men claimed to have had previous interactions with him in the Pec area and to have recognized him clearly that day. Although she didn't know his name, a third witness recognized Kastratovic from Exhibit

Photo 1 as a member of the Serbian forces in Cuska on May 14. This matches the general testimony of other witnesses who claimed that the security forces moved on to Zahac and nearby Pavljan after the killings in Cuska.

Many other people in the villages and Pec identified Vidomir Salipur in Exhibit Photo 6 (back row, center, with cap) and Exhibit Photo 7 (front row, on left, with cap) as a Pec policeman who was notorious for his use of torture and beatings against ethnic Albanians in the area. However, Salipur, who allegedly headed a local militia group called "Munja" (or Lightning), was killed by the KLA on April 11, 1999 (see Salipur's death announcement, Exhibit Photo 8), a month before the May 14 incident in Cuska.

In the process of the Cuska investigation, two people independently identified Nebojsa Minic (a.k.a. Mrtvi, or "Death") from Exhibit Photo 6 (back row, far right) and others said he was well known in the Pec area for his criminal activity. Although Minic was not seen in Cuska, the two witnesses directly implicated him in the extortion and killing of six family members from Pec on June 12. In Exhibit Photo 6, Minic is standing next to Salipur (back row, center), suggesting that the two men might have collaborated in the same militia group, possibly the group known as Munja.

The motivation for the killing in Cuska, as well as the attacks that same day on Pavljan and Zahac, remains unclear. There is no evidence to suggest any KLA presence in the villages in 1998 or 1999, and no policemen or soldiers are known to have died in the immediate vicinity during the NATO bombing, which might have made revenge a possible motive. One explanation offered by local villagers is that Cuska was the home of Hasan Ceku, the father of Agim Ceku, the military head of the KLA. Hasan and his brother, Kadri, were both killed on May 14.

Motivation aside, the killings in Cuska, Zahac, and Pavljan were closely coordinated. This was not random violence by a rogue element in the Serbian security forces. As in other villages throughout Kosovo during the war, the Yugoslav Army maintained security on the periphery of the fighting, installing checkpoints on roads leading out, while special police forces and paramilitaries went into the villages to kill and "cleanse." Whether the principal perpetrators in Cuska were a local militia, a special police unit, or perhaps both, there is no question that they were working in concert with the local police and military authorities.

There is also evidence of Yugoslav Army involvement in the attack. A number of sources reported seeing documents from the army regarding a military buildup around Cuska shortly before May 14. One international journalist claimed to have seen Yugoslav Army documents that ordered the village to be "cleansed."

Srecko Popovic   Slavisa Kastravtovic

EXHIBIT PHOTO 2

Srecko Popovic

Презиме и име......CVETKOVIC ZVONIMIR
Nom et prénom

Дан, месец и година рођења...21.11.1953
Date de naissance

Место и општина рођења......PEC
Lieu de naissance et commune

PEC

Пребивалиште и адреса стана......PEC
Domicile habituel et adresse exacte

UL.M.SAHARA BR.37

Матични број......211195393 0017
Nº d'immatriculation

(Својеручни потпис — Signature du titulaire)

CE 555770

2

3

EXHIBIT PHOTO 6

Vidomir Salipur   Nebojsa Minic

Vidomir Salipur

Са дубоком тугом обавештавамо родбину
и пријатеље да је наш драги

✝

Шалипур Видомир - "Муња"

(1970 - 1999)

јуначки погинуо бранећи Свету Српску земљу 8. априла 1999.год.
у својој 29 години живота, од руке шиптарских терориста.
Сахрана ће се обавити 11. априла (на Ускрс) на гробљу
у Добриловићима у 13 часова.
Поворка креће испред породичне куће.

Ожалошћени: *отац Ненад, мајка Рајка*
супруга Снежана, син Петар
браћа Милутин, Владан и Станко
снајке Биљана и Душица
братићи Виктор и Лазар
и остала многобројна родбина и пријатељи

ПОСЛЕДЊИ ПОЗДРАВ ОД КОЛЕГА И СТАРЕШИНА ИЗ ЈЕДИНИЦА "ОПГ" и "ПЈП" - СУП-а ПЕЋ

BACKGROUND

Cuska is a small village about five miles east of Pec near the main Pec—Pristina road; it had approximately 200 houses and 2,000 residents. Three ethnic Serbian families lived in the village, each named Jasovic, as well as one Montenegrin family named Bojovic. Relations between the Serbs and Albanians were good, the ethnic Albanian villagers said. All of the non-ethnic Albanian families left Kosovo when the Serbian and Yugoslav forces withdrew from the province on June 12.[1]

According to villagers, there was never any KLA activity in Cuska, Zahac, or Pavljan, although some of the military-age men in the area were admittedly members of the KLA who fought in the Pec municipality. The immediate Cuska area was not the scene of any fighting between government forces and the KLA in 1998 or 1999. The only incident occurred in Zahac on December 22, 1998, when the police killed one ethnic Albanian man, Sali Kabashi, and arrested five others in disputed circumstances. The Serbian government said the police came under fire during the arrest,[2] but ethnic Albanian sources claimed that Kabashi was summarily executed.[3]

During the NATO bombing of Yugoslavia in 1999, Cuska, Zahac, and Pavljan were initially left relatively untouched even though most of the surrounding villages and the city of Pec were systematically "cleansed" beginning on March 25. By March 29, more than 90 percent of Pec's population had been sent to Montenegro in the north by foot or to Albania in the southwest by bus. Other villages along the Pec–Pristina road were also vacated of ethnic Albanians in March and April, except for Cuska, Zahac, and Pavljan. Why they were not "cleansed" at this time is unknown. One unproven theory is that the villagers were paying protection money to the local security forces.

Special police forces came to Cuska three times before the May 14 attack to demand weapons and money, and they burned a few houses, but nobody was injured or killed, and everyone was allowed to stay. The first visit was April 17 around 4:00 p.m., and the forces only entered the Kristal neighborhood of the village. Between four and seven houses were burned, villagers told Human Rights Watch.

Four days later, at around 12:00 noon on April 21, security forces entered Cuska, Zahac, and Pavljan. Witnesses told Human Rights Watch that the men were in green camouflage uniforms, and some of them had green cowboy hats. Villagers also said that the forces told them not to worry. "All of you can go home. No one will touch you. You're safe," they reportedly said. The forces came again the following day and searched Cuska for weapons. A number of witnesses said that some villagers had handed over some guns they had in their possession at this time. Syle Gashi reportedly handed over a hunting rifle and his brother gave a

1 For documentation of abuses against non-ethnic Albanians after the war, see Human Rights Watch report, *Abuses Against Serbs and Roma in the New Kosovo*, August 1999.

2 Website of the Serbian Secretary of Information (www.serbia-info.com), "Albanian Terrorism after Milosevic-Holbrooke Accord," February 25, 1999, and BBC Worldwide Monitoring, Serbian Radio, "Serbia: Shoot-out Reported in Pec as Police Arrest Six Albanians," December 22, 1998.

3 The Centre for the Protection of Women and Children, *War Chronicle of the Week*, December 22, 1998.

4 Agim Ceku, a former Brigadier General in the Croatian Army, was named head of the KLA's General Staff in April 1999. In September 1999, he became the head of the newly formed Kosovo Protection Corps, the successor to the Kosovo Liberation Army.

5 Human Rights Watch interview with A.A., Ulcin, Montenegro, June 15, 1999.

6 Testimony of Ceku family members, Lawyers Committee for Human Rights, Witness Project, *Massacre in Qyshk të Pejës, Kosovo*. See the Witness Project website: www.witness.org.

pistol, as did Brahim Lushi, even though he possessed a gun license. The police also reportedly took Syle Gashi's BMW car and 1,200 DM.

Though the motive for the May 14 killings remains unclear, villagers speculate that they were targeted because Cuska was the home of Hasan Ceku, father of the KLA's chief military leader, Agim Ceku.[4] One villager claimed that the security forces on May 14 showed her a photo of Agim Ceku and said, "We are doing this because of him."[5] This is supported by testimony given to the Lawyers Committee for Human Rights, a U.S.-based human rights group. In video footage taken by the committee's Witness Project, members of the Ceku family testify that the security forces specifically asked for Agim Ceku's father, Hasan, before killing him.[6]

The police action on May 14 was clearly "more aggressive" than on previous visits, many villagers said. From the beginning, it was clear that the forces' objectives and orders went beyond a routine search for weapons.

THE KILLINGS IN CUSKA (QYSHK)

The May 14 offensive began without warning around 7:30 a.m. when a large force believed to be special police and paramilitaries entered Cuska from the direction of Pec. Villagers told Human Rights Watch that they heard automatic gunfire at about that time and saw some houses on the edge of the village being burned. Many of the young and middle-aged men fled in fear into the nearby hills, as they had during the previous police visits to Cuska, although some decided to stay with their families.

The police swept from west to east, forcing people toward the center of the village. Some villagers went willingly to the center since, as one woman said, they thought they were being expelled to Albania and "it would be safer to assemble in one place." [7] Twelve men were killed at this time in various parts of the village, including Hasan Ceku.

The Witness Project of the Lawyers Committee for Human Rights interviewed two witnesses to Hasan Ceku's killing. Both of them testified about the incident on video, the transcript of which was made available to Human Rights Watch. One witness said:

> They [the security forces] then asked who was the father of Agim Ceku, that he was big now, that we brought NATO to them, now they will eliminate us... They took Hasan, twice they let him go, and released the cattle. When he came back the last time, they had even stabbed one of the cows. They shot Hasan right there, and set him on fire. I snuck close by and saw Hasan dead, with his legs on fire. [8]

Another witness testified to the Witness Project:

> We knew that they were killing the families of Albanian officers. I believed it was just a matter of time before they killed us all. They separated us, not knowing who Agim's father was, and asking about it. [Hasan] came forward. They told him to take his family and separated us. They took [Hasan] to find a picture of Agim, while they questioned me and my sister-in-law. They asked us when was the last time we saw him [Agim]. Where? But we had already decided that no matter what, we would never admit that we have any contact with him. I was telling him never. At that moment [Hasan] brought the picture, in which I was with Agim. He recognized me, but I denied it. He told me I was lucky because I was carrying a little child with me. They asked me to follow them and tell them whose house was the one across the street. Then I heard the shots. I ran but my uncle did not let me see [Hasan] dead. [9]

7 Human Rights Watch interview with A.A., Ulcin, Montenegro, June 15, 1999.

8 Testimony of Ceku family members, Lawyers Committee for Human Rights, Witness Project, *Massacre in Qyshk të Pejës, Kosovo*. See the Witness Project website at www.witness.org.

9 Ibid.

10 Human Rights Watch
interview with B.B., Cuska,
July 15, 1999.

11 Human Rights Watch
interview with A.A., Ulcin,
Montenegro, June 15, 1999.

12 Human Rights Watch
interview with B.B., Cuska,
July 15, 1999.

Despite these initial killings, some men decided to stay with their families. One 38-year-old man, B.B., remained with approximately forty people from his family, including his mother and children. He explained to Human Rights Watch:

> When I saw them [the Serbian forces] near my house they looked very aggressive, so I decided to run. Down the road I saw some young men who told me they [the Serbian forces] had killed three men. I decided to come to the neighborhood of the Gashi family. When I got there I spoke with some old men who had decided to wait for the military to come. Right after that, the Lushi and Kelmendi families came—women, men, and children.[10]

B.B. and other villagers interviewed separately told Human Rights Watch that a group of approximately 200 ethnic Albanians from the village was soon surrounded by an estimated one-hundred security forces. All of the witnesses said that the forces were wearing green military-style uniforms. All of them had their faces covered in some way, either with black grease paint or a mask, and some of them had black scarves and green cowboy-style hats.

All of the villagers believed that some of the security forces were from the Pec area, such as the ethnic Serbian village of Gorazdevac (Gorazhdefc), which is across the Bistrica River from Cuska. Some of the forces seemed to know a few of the local Albanians personally, villagers told Human Rights Watch, since they asked for specific valuables, such as the "car keys to your Mercedes." One woman who was in close contact with the forces told Human Rights Watch:

> They wore green camouflage uniforms. Most of them had handkerchiefs around their heads, and two of them had hats, but some of them had their heads uncovered. All of them had their faces painted. We could only see their eyes, so we could not recognize them. But it was obvious that some of them knew us. There is a very short man from Cuska, a drunkard, whom people make fun of. Some soldiers started making fun of him, and from the way they did it, it was clear they knew him... Also, some of the soldiers would say to a person: "Get the keys of your Mercedes!" or "Give us the keys to your van!" That is, they knew who was who and who owned what.[11]

B.B. told Human Rights Watch:

> I think they were from around here because they knew the men by name and they told them to get their cars. I recognized some of their faces. [12]

For more details on the identities of the security forces, see the section on perpetrators in this chapter.

After the crowd of villagers was concentrated in the village center, thirty-two men were separated from the women and children. The entire group was then systematically robbed of their valuables. B.B. explained:

They ordered us to empty our pockets of all valuables—money, jewelry, gold. After they finished that, they ordered two kids, aged thirteen and fourteen. One was to take our IDs and the other to collect the valuables. The man who [later] executed us put a knife to the childrens' throats and said "give us everything you have." They shot near the kids' legs and above their heads.[13]

C.C., 57 years old, was also captured as he tried to leave his house and forced to gather in the village center. He told Human Rights Watch:

The wife of my brother was twenty meters away. They told her to stop and they put a machine gun to her neck. They took about 850 DM from her. One of them cursed me and hit me in the face with his hand. "What do you think, you will never have a democracy," they said. "This is Serbia. America or NATO have no business here."

They took us to the cemetery. The Gashi, Lushi, and Kelmendi families were there, along with some guests from Lodza, Graboc, Rausic, and Gorazdevac... They started to separate the women, children, and old men from the younger men. I didn't recognize them because at that moment most of them were masked or with black color on their faces. They stole from us; from me they took about 200 DM. They took our watches, documents, some of which they burned, our gold, and jewelry.[14]

Another woman who was present, D.D., told Human Rights Watch that the women and children stayed in the village center for approximately one hour. She said:

The soldiers were taking things from us: money, cigarettes, watches, jewelry... One soldier took a knife and started licking it. He put it under the throat of a child. One of my children, my three-year-old son, broke free from my hands and started running to the direction of the group of men, where my husband was. The soldiers shot into the ground close to my son's legs to stop him.[15]

Another woman, A.A., corroborated this account. She added:

We [the women] stayed at the square. A soldier told us that they had an order to kill all of the villagers, but that they would spare women and children. He asked: "Do you want us to take you to Albania or to Montenegro?" We did not answer.[16]

After stripping everyone of their documents and valuables, the security forces separated twelve men from the group of thirty-two and brought them into a yard between the houses of Ajet and Haki Gashi. The twelve men were led into the nearby house of Syle Gashi. What happened next is best described by the testimony of C.C., who was in the group:

Four of them came with us, three soldiers and one policeman. One had an automatic machine gun with two legs and the other three had normal machine guns. They put us near the wall. One of them was at the door with the machine

13 Ibid.

14 Human Rights Watch interview with C.C., Cuska, July 16, 1999.

15 Human Rights Watch interview with D.D., Rozaje, Montenegro, June 8, 1999.

16 Human Rights Watch interview with A.A., Ulcin, Montenegro, June 15, 1999.

151

17 Human Rights Watch
Interview with C.C., Cuska,
July 16, 1999.

gun—a young soldier. He said, "We will execute all of your families at the cemetery. You'll give us all your money if you want to be saved." We said we didn't have any more money and you can do anything you want with us.

Then he said he would talk with his colleagues to see what he'd do with us. They spoke by walkie-talkie with their commander but I didn't hear what they said. At once he stepped into the door with the machine gun. We were against the wall with our hands up. He said, "In the name of Serbia you will all be shot."

Ibro [Iber] Kelmendi was on the left side. He has a weak heart and when he heard what he said, he died and fell on top of me. I pretended like I was dead too. Then he opened fire and everyone was killed except one guy. He shot once more at that person—I don't know who it was. I was wounded too, in the upper leg. Another guy came and shot again, then a third guy emptied his machine gun, then the fourth. I was alive under Ibro Kelmendi and my brother.

They cursed Albanians and then they set the house on fire. They broke a window and lit the stuffing from a mattress and put it over the bodies. I pushed the bodies aside and got out. I decided it was better to kill me than to be burned alive, so I jumped out the window. I went 100 meters and hid. I hid from 10:00 a.m. to 5:00 p.m.[17]

Human Rights Watch inspected Syle Gashi's house on July 16. Only the walls were standing, and the interior had been completely burned. Small fragments of bone were scattered among the charred roof tiles and wooden beams that lay on the ground.

B.B. was among the men waiting outside the garden gate. He told Human Rights Watch that he heard shooting two or three minutes after the first group had been taken away, and he knew they had been killed. He told Human Rights Watch

The police returned, talked among themselves and asked some young boys around fifteen and sixteen to go with the women and children. Then they separated us into two groups. When they took us [eleven men], one guy didn't know which way to go and they hit him with a gun and said "Go this way!" They told us to go with our hands on our head and walk quickly. When we came here [house of Sahit Gashi], one said, "put them here." Another said, "It's not good to put them here because it will smell." So we went to Sahit Gashi's house. First they said stand near the bathroom. I first thought they would execute us there but one guy with many bullets on his chest—12.7 mm—said, "No, go in this room." They were very calm. They cursed us but they were not shouting. I wonder how they can kill us when they are so calm.

We went into the kitchen. I saw the fire from the machine gun and I fell to my left. I think everyone was killed but I wasn't even wounded. He sprayed three times. The same man went to the other side of the room and shot again at those who had fallen. Three times again. One bullet hit me in the leg. I was hit on my left leg below the knee. Then I was hit on the right leg above the knee. The third

bullet hit me in the right shin and broke the bone.[18]

Then he took out his pistol and shot six or seven people but I wasn't watching because my eyes were closed. Then everything stopped. There was silence. I waited for two or three minutes and slowly opened my eyes. When I saw no one was around I looked to my right and saw Isuf Shala was dead. Arian Lushi was dead on my right. The others were dead too. I saw five police from the window and I heard one of them coming. I stayed lying down with my eyes half closed watching what he was doing. He just put his head in the room and threw something and very quickly some black smoke started going from that. After a few seconds, I couldn't breathe. When I thought I was going to scream because I was choking, I was thinking "please God, help" and I got up and went to the door. I thought I'd be killed but it is very hard to be burned alive.

I went to the other room and jumped from the window. I jumped out and saw their cars. One had a big Gulinov. They had civilian vehicles, trucks, and tractors and military vehicles too.[19]

Like Syle Gashi's house, Sahit Gashi's home was also burnt out, with only the walls remaining, when visited by Human Rights Watch on July 15.

E.E. was in the last group of nine men waiting outside the garden gate. In a brief interview with Human Rights Watch he confirmed that his group had been taken into Deme Gashi's house and was shot there. He survived uninjured. During the discussion, however, the photographs of his deceased family members and neighbors arrived for use in the ceremonial service that was planned to take place in Cuska the next day, July 18, rendering the moment improper for an in-depth interview.

Some foreign journalists, however, did speak in detail with E.E. about his experience. In an article published in the June 28 edition of *Time* magazine, the survivor is quoted about what happened after the security forces took him into the two-story house:

> **I was together with eight others. When we entered the hallway of the house, one of the VJ [Yugoslav Army] soldiers gave us a lighter and told us to burn down the house. When I bent down to take the lighter, the shooting started. I started crawling, not lifting my head.[20]**

Human Rights Watch also spoke with E.E.'s niece, A.A., in Montenegro where she was a refugee. She told Human Rights Watch that she had met her uncle near Cuska the night of May 14 and relayed what he had said to her at that time:

> **At twilight, our uncle E.E. came and told us that the men had been separated into three groups and led into three houses. He was the first to enter one of the houses. He was given a lighter by a soldier and ordered to light a curtain in the room. When he kneeled down to set the curtain on fire, he heard a machine gun burst. He jumped out of the window and ran away.[21]**

18 Human Rights Watch saw what appeared to be bullet scars below the witness's left knee and above his right knee. At the time of interview, the witness was still wearing a cast from his right knee down to his ankle.

19 Human Rights Watch interview with B.B., Cuska, July 15, 1999.

20 "Kosovo Crisis— The Awful Truth," *Time*, June 28, 1999.

21 Human Rights Watch interview with A.A., Ulcin, Montenegro, June 15, 1999.

22 Ibid.

23 Human Rights Watch
interview with D.D., Rozaje,
Montenegro, June 8, 1999.

24 Human Rights Watch
interview with F.F., Pec, July
15, 1999.

The events described by the three survivors were corroborated by other individuals in Cuska on May 14, including the women who were in close proximity to the security forces before being sent out of the village around the time the first group of men was being led into Syle Gashi's house. As they were leaving, they heard shots, some of them said, but they were not able to determine where they came from. A.A. told Human Rights Watch:

While we were leaving Cuska, the soldiers started shooting in our direction, but they were only shooting into the ground. Because of the noise and the fear we felt, we were unable to discern precisely what was shot at, and all the places the shooting was coming from. Maybe there was some other shooting as well at the same time, but we were not able to discern it.[22]

The women and children in the village were loaded onto tractors and escorted by the Serbian forces to the nearby Trepca battery factory on the Pec–Pristina road. One woman in the group told Human Rights Watch that they met the commander of the Pec-Klicina police station at a checkpoint near the factory. He was apparently surprised to see the women and children, asked who had sent them there, and returned them in the direction of Cuska, accompanied by men in three civilian cars, a gray Audi and two Zastavas. D.D. said:

The soldiers set Sali's house on fire. The roof began to fall. Then they put us on tractors and horses. Around 10:00 a.m. they took us—women, children, and several old men—in front of the Trepca factory, which is between Cuska and the center of Pec. While we were leaving, we heard gunfire. The soldiers didn't say much on the way to the factory.

We stayed for four hours in front of Trepca. The police there told us to go back to Cuska. When we got close to the village, we saw the burnt houses. I entered the house of Ram Binaku. I saw burnt bodies in one of the rooms. Most of the bodies were impossible to recognize. The woman recognized pieces of things belonging to their husbands, such as lighters, watches, keys... I think Skender Dervishi [Lushi] was burned alive, because next to his body I saw traces in the ground, as if somebody was scratching his hand in the surface. I fainted.[23]

Another man, F.F., age 35, fled into the hills when the security forces arrived but returned later that day to discover many of the bodies, ultimately burying thirty-five of the forty-one victims. He told Human Rights Watch:

We went about 300 meters from the village where there is a wooded hill. We saw the burning houses and heard shooting and screaming. Then the forces went away. About thirty or forty-five minutes later, [E.E.] came. We saw he was not okay. I asked him what happened. He couldn't speak a word but just replied, "What happened to us. What happened to us" while putting his hands on his head. He looked inhuman.[24]

E.E. told the men in the hills that people had been killed in the village but he was too traumatized to explain, F.F. said. About an hour later, F.F. and another man

154

named Ajet went into Cuska to see what happened. On the way, they saw Zoran Jasovic, an ethnic Serb civilian who lived in Cuska, waving a Yugoslav flag in front of a burning house, apparently to let the security forces know that he was Serbian. He didn't see the ethnic Albanian men and then he left the area. F.F. explained what happened next:

> He [Jasovic] left and we went to that house. I went inside and saw the bodies burning. It was the house of Deme Gashi. I didn't identify them or count them. We went back to the woods and invited Sadik Gashi to come with us. We went back and tried to put the fire out. The forces had left at that time. None of our family members were around....
>
> I saw the burning house of Syle Gashi and we saw a large number of burning victims. I cannot tell how many people were there, it's better to speak with an eyewitness. I decided to inspect each house. In the house of Ahmet Gashi we found burning bodies but we couldn't put out the flames. In Ajet's house we saw two other burning bodies: Syle Gashi and Skender Gashi... Then we went to Sali Gashi's house. We saw the body of Ibish Gashi with many bullet holes. We saw an outhouse near the road riddled with bullets. I opened the door slowly, very slowly, and I saw Qaush Lushi dead. He was killed with a 7.9 mm machine gun.

Human Rights Watch inspected the outhouse where Qaush Lushi was reportedly killed. It was a small wooden structure on the side of the road with ten bullet holes in the front door, and nine bullet holes on the far wall inside. Danish forensic experts who were coincidentally examining the site at the time for the International Criminal Tribunal for the former Yugoslavia told Human Rights Watch that they had gathered positive evidence of human blood inside. Two bullets were found, they said, one inside the outhouse and one wedged into the wood. They appeared to be 7.6 mm caliber.[25]

Villagers in Cuska told Human Rights Watch that Qaush Lushi was the richest man in the village, and that he had been forced to give the police 10,000 DM before he and his son, Arian, were killed. An article in *Time* magazine covering the killings in Cuska also said that Lushi returned from his house with money for the police to find his son already dead. He was then forced into the outhouse where he was killed.[26]

B.B. confirmed that the police had targeted Qaush Lushi. He told Human Rights Watch:

> They [the security forces] said "Do you want a state? We are 11 million Serbs so if you want a state ask for help from Clinton and Blair. Ask for NATO's help now." Qaush said, "We have a state." And one of them said, "While I was defending you, you got rich." Two times they took Qaush to his home and when he went to this garden [near Azem Gashi's house], they shot above his head. Qaush came back with his car.[27]

25 Human Rights Watch interview, Cuska, July 15, 1999.

26 "Kosovo Crisis— The Awful Truth," *Time*, June 28, 1999.

27 Human Rights Watch interview with B.B., Cuska, July 15, 1999.

28 Human Rights Watch interview with F.F., Pec, July 15, 1999.

F.F. told Human Rights Watch what happened the next day, May 15, after he and other villagers had spent the night in the forest:

> **The next day, the families who had slept in the Kelmendi house, Ajet, Milaim, and me, decided to bury the bodies because we didn't want the families to see them in that condition. I proposed and we decided to dig one mass grave because it was too dangerous to take the time digging many graves. Some women and children came and realized that their men had been killed and burned. They asked me "where is so and so." I said, "everyone who is not here is dead."**
>
> **We found thirty-one burned bodies and buried them with two unburned bodies, that of Ibish Gashi and Qaush Lushi... [The next day] it rained very hard. We decided that we, Skender, Ajet, Milaim, and me would go and take two other bodies, one near my house, with a stretcher and we saw one old man who was watching the body of my uncle Brahim, who was killed by a bullet to the heart. We took him to the grave site. We went to look for our neighbor Rasim... We found Rasim in his garden. He had been killed by many bullets. In his garden had been another executed person, Mete [Muhamet] Shala, but he had already been taken by his brother.[28]**

By mid-afternoon, the group of women, children, and elderly had been sent back to Cuska. Uniformed men put people from three families—Lushi, Gashi, and Kelmendi—into the house of Shaban Binaku. They, and those who had managed to escape the attack, stayed in the village or the nearby forest until the end of the war.

THE PERPETRATORS

From the beginning of the Kosovo armed conflict in late February 1998, ethnic Albanians in Kosovo were rarely able to identify the perpetrators of human rights abuses against them. On occasion, a specific individual or police chief was recognized, but witnesses and victims generally refer to abusers in generic terms like "the paramilitaries" or "soldiers."

One reason is the complex combination of forces that were active in the province, including regular Yugoslav Army soldiers, military police, army special forces, the regular Serbian police, anti-terrorist units of the police, special police forces, state security special forces, paramilitary groups, international mercenaries, and armed local Serbs, all of which were coordinated by Belgrade. The various forces often used interchangeable uniforms; pants, shirts, and jackets were mixed and matched, perhaps to avoid identification. Insignias were not always displayed, and name tags or identification numbers were never visible.

Kosovo fell under the jurisdiction of the Yugoslav Army's Third Army, commanded during the war by Col. Gen. Nebojsa Pavkovic. The commander of the Pristina Corps based in Kosovo was Maj. Gen. Vladimir Lazarevic. The main organ of the Yugoslav Army is the General Staff, headed during the 1999 war by Gen. Dragoljub Ojdanic. His direct superior and Supreme Commander of the army was then-Yugoslav president Slobodan Milosevic.

As described in the appendix on chain of command, Kosovo fell under the jurisdiction of the Serbian Ministry of the Interior, run during the war by Minister Vlajko Stojiljkovic, had a strong presence in the province, including the regular police, the special police (Posebne Jedinice Policije, or PJP), the special anti-terrorist forces (Specijalna Antiteroristicka Jedinica, or SAJ), and the Special Operations Unit (Jedinica za Specijalne Operacije, or JSO) of the state security service (Sluzba Drzavne Bezbednosti, or SDB).

In addition, paramilitaries and "volunteers" were active in Kosovo during 1999, mostly integrated into the army or the police. Aside from being among the most violent forces in Kosovo, responsible for many of the killings and rapes, one of their primary activities was looting and theft. There may have been specific incidents where paramilitary units or individuals got out of control, but the general deployment of paramilitary units and their coordination with other sectors of the Serbian and Yugoslav security apparatus were planned components of the Kosovo campaign.

Abuses in the Pec area offer new possibilities for perpetrator identification, since, unlike in other parts of Kosovo, the local Albanians had regular contact on a variety of levels with the many ethnic Serbs who lived in the area. Pec itself, seat of the Serbian Orthodox Church, had a sizable Serbian population, as did some of the area's villages, such as Gorazdevac and Nakle (Nakille).

In Cuska, many of the local Albanians believed that the security forces who were in the village on May 14 included ethnic Serbs from the area. As described in the section on the killings, the security forces seemed to know some of the individual Albanians, such as the wealthy Qaush Lushi, even asking them to hand over very specific valuables, such as "the keys to your Mercedes," and they teased a local drunkard. Other villagers told Human Rights Watch that the forces spoke Serbian with a clear Kosovo accent, as opposed to Serbs from southern Serbia or Belgrade. One villager in Pavljan said she recognized some of the forces in her village as Serbs from the area, although she knew no names. "One of them worked as a doorman where they sell cheese and milk in Llomae Bilmetit," she said.[29] D.D. from Cuska told Human Rights Watch:

> **We recognized four [ethnic Serbian] men who were from Gorazdevac. Boban was the leader of the group, he is from Gorazdevac too. He had a beard. He was the one with a hat.[30]**

B.B. told Human Rights Watch:

> **I think they were from around here because they knew the men by name and they told them to get their cars. I recognized some of their faces.[31]**

C.C. said he recognized some of the men who came on the third visit to Cuska, just before the May 14 killing. He told Human Rights Watch:

> **There were three brothers from Nakle with a father named Blagoj. Their mother was born and used to live in Cuska. Her father is Zivajlevic. Her name was Darinka. Some of them, two of them, were from Zahac... Two were from Pec, one was Srdjan, the other Boban.[32]**

In numerous interviews with villagers, a number of physical descriptions emerged. One woman, H.H., described the man she thought was a commander in Cuska (because he spoke on a walkie-talkie) as approximately six feet tall, slightly fat and age 40. He had short black hair, shaved on the sides, with a bit of white on the top, she said. He had a beard that was speckled with gray and he wore an army uniform with no hat.[33] Other villagers also described the commander as having a light beard. B.B. told Human Rights Watch:

> **One guy with a short beard with grey speckles looked like a commander because he gave the orders.[34]**

The most damning evidence, however, is from witness identifications using a series of twenty-one photographs obtained by Human Rights Watch that depict armed and uniformed men who were apparently in some form of military unit or units, either police reservists, special forces, a local militia, or paramilitaries. Two individuals in the photographs were positively identified by multiple witnesses as having been present in Cuska on May 14, and a third person was seen in Zahac on the same day. A number of other individuals were identified, al-though they were not in Cuska on May 14, and some were not identified at all.

Human Rights Watch obtained the photographs on July 16 from the municipal administration in Pec, which was run at that time by former members of the KLA, including Ethem Ceku, cousin of Agim Ceku. The photographs depict various

29 Human Rights Watch interview with G.G., Pavljan, July 17, 1999.

30 Human Rights Watch interview with D.D., Rozaje, Montenegro, June 8, 1999.

31 Human Rights Watch interview with B.B., Cuska, July 15, 1999.

32 Human Rights Watch interview with C.C., Cuska, July 16, 1999.

33 Human Rights Watch interview with H.H., Cuska, July 16, 1999.

34 Human Rights Watch interview with B.B., Cuska, July 15, 1999.

35 One of the people who identified the man as a commander also claimed that he had taken her away into a home, apparently with the aim to rape her. According to the woman, the man told her she knew what she had to do to save her family. For an unknown reason, she was then let go.

The following photographs on pages 163 - 165 are of the man identified as Srecko Popovic.

individuals and groups in an assortment of military poses. Some show men in military uniforms posing in a field or village. Others have men in full military outfits and automatic guns in front of burning houses or displaying the three-fingered Serbian nationalist salute. The KLA officials told Human Rights Watch that the photographs had been found in the homes of ethnic Serbian citizens in the Pec area after Serbian and Yugoslav forces withdrew from Kosovo on June 12. Human Rights Watch also obtained two other group photographs dated May 6, 1999, of what, from the shoulder insignia, appears to be special police forces, from villagers in Zahac. The villagers told Human Rights Watch that they had found the photographs in the home of an ethnic Serb in Nakle.

A Human Rights Watch researcher scanned all of the photographs into a laptop computer and then showed them to villagers in Cuska, Zahac, and Pavljan, as well as to people in Pec, to see if anyone recognized or could identify any of the individuals. The methodology employed was to show the photographs one by one to only a single person at a time, preferably in a one-on-one setting.

Human Rights Watch cannot confirm the authenticity of the photographs, because their origin, method of procurement, and ownership record are unknown. The fact that they were provided by the KLA, in whose interest it is to identify Serbian war criminals, should heighten suspicion about their accuracy. But, even if the photographs were doctored, there is no question that the villagers interviewed by Human Rights Watch positively identified some of the people in the photographs, and it is out of the question that this was coordinated between them and the KLA. Human Rights Watch asked the KLA for the photographs, rather than receiving them on the KLA's initiative, and did not mention that they would be shown to villagers in the area.

The results of Human Rights Watch's investigation are as follows. One man was recognized by six different people, interviewed separately, who said they had seen him in Cuska on May 14. Five of these people identified him from Exhibit Photo 1 (second from left), and only one of these people qualified this, saying "I am 90 percent sure he was here." The others were emphatic in their answers. Two of the interviewees said the man in the photographs was a commander in Cuska on May 14, and one other who had also placed him there said he "might be the commander," that is, a person who was directing the others in the group and talking on a walkie-talkie.**35**

Exhibit Photos 2 (man on right) and 3 appear to show the same person, although cleanly shaven. One of the five witnesses who recognized the man from Exhibit Photo 1 said the same man was on the right in Exhibit Photos 2 and 3, and that the other security forces had called him "Popa." One further witness, who did not react to Exhibit Photo 1, said that the man on the right in Exhibit Photo 2 was in Cuska on May 14, and that he had gone to Deme Gashi's house where nine people were killed. "He had no beard," she said. When viewing Exhibit Photo 3, the witness claimed that the man had visited Cuska with the Serbian forces in April, and that he had worn a beard at that time. By her account, he "waved his assault rifle and said 'you can't run from this.'"

Aside from having heard the nickname "Popa," none of these witnesses knew the man's name when they identified him in the photographs: they only claimed that

36 Human Rights Watch later interviewed the same ethnic Albanian who, without suggestion, identified the same man in Exhibit Photo 3 as Srecko Popovic.

37 For more information from the American RadioWorks report, including photographs, see their website at www.americanradioworks.org

38 Smith and Montgomery later confronted Cvetkovic personally in Montenegro. He denied having been in Cuska or having ever donned a military uniform.

39 Human Rights Watch interview with I.I., Zahac, July 22, 1999.

The photograph on page 167 shows the man identified as Slavisa Kastratovic (middle).

he had been in Cuska. His name, Srecko Popovic, had been provided previously to Human Rights Watch by the local KLA, but it was later confirmed by two U.S. journalists who were also investigating war crimes in the Pec area and using the same set of photographs to identify perpetrators. According to Stephen Smith and Michael Montgomery from American RadioWorks, whose radio series on Cuska and war crimes in Kosovo generally has aired on National Public Radio's "All Things Considered" in the United States throughout 2000 and 2001, the three men they interviewed—one ethnic Albanian and two ethnic Serbs—identified Popovic by name when they saw Exhibit Photo 3. [36] In addition, Smith and Montgomery found another five people who didn't know Popovic's name but placed him in Cuska on May 14. Two of these people considered Popovic a commander. [37]

Another man identified as being in Cuska on May 14 is Zvonimir (Zvonko) Cvetkovic. The strongest witness claimed to have seen Cvetkovic in Cuska on that day, and even to have spoken with him. The witness identified him immediately from the group photograph of the men in front of the truck, Exhibit Photo 4 (Cvetkovic on far right), saying, "Of course I know Zvonko. We lived on the same street." Human Rights Watch later obtained a copy of Cvetkovic's passport that was found in the Petrans trucking company in Pec where he worked. The passport photo (Exhibit Photo 5) appears to match the man on the right in the group picture. Another man, F.F., separately told Human Rights Watch that he had seen Zvonko Cvetkovic in Cuska on May 14, but he admitted to only learning his name later, and he did not see the photographs in Human Rights Watch's possession. Smith and Montgomery, however, had two other people separately identify Cvetkovic by name from the passport photograph. Both people claimed to have seen him in Cuska on May 14. [38]

Based on these identifications, Human Rights Watch believes there is strong evidence to place both Srecko Popovic and Zvonko Cvetkovic in Cuska on May 14. We do not have evidence, however, that either of these men participated directly in the execution of the forty-one men. It can only be said that they were present with the security forces when these executions, as well as the burning of homes and the theft of private property, took place. In the very least, they possess valuable information about the war crimes that were committed, including the names of commanders, and they should, therefore, be the subject of an investigation by the International Criminal Tribunal for the former Yugoslavia.

Two other ethnic Albanian men from Zahac, interviewed separately, said they recognized Slavisa Kastratovic in Exhibit Photo 1 (middle), next to Srecko Popovic) as a member of the security forces present in Zahac on May 14. One of the men, who claimed to have had regular contact with local Serbs through his job, said that Kastravtovic was from Gorazdevac and that he had worked in the Pik Trading Company. The other man claimed to have known Kastratovic personally. He told Human Rights Watch:

> **On May 14, I saw Slavisa Kastratovic. He spoke with me. He asked how I am. "I'm glad your sons are alive," he said. I only have young kids.**[39]

Another person from Cuska, H.H., recognized Kastratovic from Exhibit Photo 1 as having been in Cuska on May 14, although she did not know his name. She told

Human Rights Watch that he had been in Cuska that day, as well as on previous occasions in April when the security forces had checked the village.[40] The testimony of the three witnesses from Cuska and Zahac provides some evidence that the same forces were involved in the actions in both places on May 14.

The other name that came up repeatedly in interviews was Vidomir Salipur, known by almost everyone in Pec and the surrounding villages simply as Salipur. Interviews and conversations with dozens of Pec residents revealed Salipur's reputation for brutality. A member of the Pec police department, he was known for eagerly beating and torturing ethnic Albanians on the street or in detention. Local human rights activists, journalists, and the KLA, as well as a number of ordinary Pec citizens told Human Rights Watch that Salipur was also the head of a local militia group or paramilitary called Munja (or "Lightning" in English), which was also Salipur's nickname.[41] The group was apparently made up of local Serbs, some of whom were in the police and others who were civilians. According to Salipur's death announcement (see Exhibit Photo 8), obtained by Human Rights Watch, he was killed by the KLA on April 8, 1999:

With great sadness we announce to family and friends that our dear

Salipur Vidomir - "The Lightning"

(1970-1999)

Died a heroic death defending the Holy Serbian land on April 8th

1999 in the 29th year of his life, at the hand of Albanian terrorists.

The funeral will take place tomorrow, April 11th (Easter), at the

Dobrilovici cemetery at 1:00 p.m.

The procession leaves in front of the family house...

LAST SALUTE FROM COLLEAGUES AND OFFICERS FROM "OPG"

AND "PJP" UNITS - PEC POLICE DEPARTMENT

The acronym PJP refers to the special police forces under the Ministry of Internal Affairs (Posebna Jedinica Policije, or Police Special Unit). OPG most likely refers to Operativna Grupa, although it is not clear how this group fit into the structure of the Serbian Ministry of the Interior. The fact that Salipur, as a Serbian policeman, was apparently in a military unit together with ethnic Serbian civilians, possibly the Munja group, suggests that the Interior Ministry knew about the activities of local militias, if it did not organize, arm, and coordinate them. Human Rights Watch obtained two photographs of Salipur together with a group of armed, uniformed men (Exhibit Photos 6 and 7). In Exhibit Photo 7, Salipur is seen crouching in the front row on the left, holding an Albanian flag. The identities of the other men are unknown.

In Exhibit Photo 6, Salipur is standing in the middle of the back row wearing a cap in front of what appears to be a flag marking the Albanian–Yugoslav border. To his left is a man identified separately by two individuals as Nebojsa Minic, who has been directly implicated as the leader of a gang that extorted and then killed

40 Human Rights Watch interview with H.H., Cuska, July 16, 1999.

41 For an article on Salipur, see "The Merciless Life and Death of a Paramilitary Killer; Sadistic Cop Tortured Town," by Paul Salopek, *Chicago Tribune*, June 27, 1999.

The photograph on page 168 shows the men identified as Vidomir Salipur (back row center) and Nebojsa Minic (back row right).

42 A gang led by Nebojsa Minic, witnesses told Human Rights Watch, entered the Pec home of a family around 9:00 p.m. and demanded money. One young woman was raped before the family was shot with automatic weapons. Six people died (ages 5, 6, 7, 12, 13, and 28) and four survived.

43 Kandic later confirmed her report directly to Human Rights Watch.

44 "Special Report, Retribution in Kosovo," *VIP Daily News Report*, Issue 1559, July 28, 1999. The Yugoslav Army's 125th Motorized Brigade, based in Kosovska, Mitrovica, and Pec, was commanded by Colonel Dragan Zivanovic.

45 "U.N. Records Link Serbs to War Crimes," by Jack Kelley, *USA Today*, July 14, 1999.

The photograph on page 171 shows the man identified as "Milan". The photographs on pages 172 - 174 show the man identified as Vidomir Salipur. On page 174 Vidomir Salipur is front row, left (with flag). The photograph on pages 176 and 177 show the man identified as Srecko Popovic (far right).

six members of one family, age 6 to 28, in Pec on June 12.[42] Two people who said they had had direct contact with Minic told Human Rights Watch that he is heavily tattooed with images of a knife, an axe, and a grenade on his forearm, and a dead man on his chest. The man in the front row of Exhibit Photo 6, far left, was identified independently by two people, as well as by KLA sources, as "Milan," allegedly a friend of Salipur's, although no specific allegations were leveled against him. The identities of the other men in the photograph are unknown.

There is also some evidence of the involvement of the Yugoslav Army (Vojska Jugoslavija, or VJ) in the attacks on Cuska, Pavljan, and Zahac. Local KLA authorities in Pec told Human Rights Watch in July that they possessed a notebook that, they claimed, belonged to an officer in the VJ. Notes in the book mentioned a military build-up in the Cuska area prior to the May 14 killing, they said.

Shortly thereafter, Natasa Kandic from the Belgrade-based Humanitarian Law Center, one of Yugoslavia's strongest human rights groups, published a report in which she mentioned the notebook of a VJ lieutenant shown to her by the KLA authorities in Pec.[43] She wrote that the book:

[R]egister[ed] the military activities in the municipality of Pec after March 24. The entry for March 11 said that the focus of military activities should be shifted to Cuska and its vicinity. The local KLA headquarters in Pec also had a document marked confidential bearing the signature of the colonel in charge of the 125th Brigade.[44]

A subsequent article in the international press claimed that the Hague Tribunal had found Yugoslav Army documents that ordered the "cleansing" of Cuska. A journalist for *USA Today* reported that he had inspected a black vinyl, three-ringed notebook that contained a direct order typed on army stationery and stamped by the Supreme Defense Council of the Yugoslav Army headquarters in Belgrade. The order reportedly said, "The aim of the military activity should be to cleanse Cuska and the surrounding villages and terrain."[45] The article said that investigators from the war crimes tribunal had found the notebook on July 2 near an abandoned military headquarters in Kosovo.

Са дубоком туго
и пријате

Шалипур В⟨

(197

јуначки погинуо бранећи Свету Срп
у својој 29 години живота, од ру
Сахрана ће се обавити 11. апри
у Добриловићима

Поворка креће испред

Ожалошћени: *отац Ненад, мајка*
супруга Снежана,
браћа Милутин, В⟨

The photographs in the photo album were found as undeveloped film in a field near Orahovac, Kosovo, in the summer of 1999 by a German journalist, who then gave them to Human Rights Watch. The remaining photographs were either obtained in July 1999 from local authorities in Kosovo's western city of Pec, whose administration was at that time run by former members of the Kosovo Liberation Army, or were provided by American RadioWorks, which has done extensive reporting on Kosovo. We believe all of these photographs were taken by members of the Serbian security forces and then left behind after their departure from Kosovo in June 1999.

Human Rights Watch collected no evidence that the persons depicted in these photographs are personally responsible for the commission of war crimes.

The excerpts in this chapter are from interviews with Serb fighters who were active in Pec and surrounding villages until NATO troops entered Kosovo in June 1999. The interviews were conducted by Michael Montgomery and Stephen Smith of American RadioWorks in Montenegro in September and November 1999. The first names in these excerpts are pseudonyms.

SELF-PORTRAITS

SNAPSHOTS BY
SERBIAN MILITARY AND
PARAMILITARY FORCES

AGFA

HIGH
DEFINITION
COLOR

AGFA *Agfa* **FILM**

HIGH
DEFINITION
COLOR FILMS

Milan is a Bosnian Serb who belonged to the militia gang Munja (Lightning).

I was recruited into Munja by a member of the Serbian Radical Party in Belgrade. He provided us with weapons, ammunition, satellite phones and walkie-talkies. That was the middle of March 1999, ten days before NATO began bombing.

We trained for three days at a camp in Leskovac (Serbia). There were 20 in my unit, and most of the guys came with war experience from Bosnia and other places. Three of them were former members of the Yugoslav state security service in Croatia. Many of them were criminals.

The goal was to fight against the KLA and to cleanse away their support. I am a Serbian patriot. I fought for the Serbian cause. And also for the sake of money. Money was the main thing.

We heard that members of the Serbian secret police were transporting Albanian civilians in the trunk of their cars for $2,700. There were some members of my unit who would take the money and just kill the guy. I didn't do such things. I took them to the border. When the NATO bombing intensified, I started doing the same thing—taking the money and killing them. (...)

[In one operation] we suspected that in four houses in the village, there were members of the KLA. I opened mortar fire on those houses and we entered the hamlet. When we arrived there were dead people; five or six civilians, a couple KLA soldiers. Those who survived, they fled to the forest. We were successful and didn't even need artillery support from the army, like the other groups.

We grabbed two wounded guys who we thought were from the KLA and killed them.

Our job was to cleanse the village. Some other villagers were hiding in the forest, so we went there to pick them up. There was this village elder, some old Albanian guy, who refused to leave. I mean the guy was just pathetic. We ordered him to go to the border to Albania, but he just refused. So we put a bullet in his forehead. The others were taken to the border while we burned everything in that village. The whole village.

We'd hear about what was happening to Serbs every day on the news. When you see that NATO is bombing the center of a town or the television station in Belgrade, and every day friends, comrades died, you don't care about the Albanians. Why would you? We lived off revenge. Sweet revenge.

Back then, revenge felt very good. Especially when we killed the KLA...Now I can't sleep, I can't eat. It hasn't lasted.

Marko was released from a Serbian prison to fight in Kosovo. He went to Pec in a unit of the Serbian warlord Zeljko Raznatovic, better known as Arkan.

I have an ugly history with Serbia. It's ugly. I don't like it there. I hate Serbia. I was in prison. I deserved what I was sentenced for...I was almost two and a half years in prison. Nobody likes war. But there were 50 of us who were offered to defend the state and in return get our freedom from prison. Well, let me tell you, that for freedom we would do just about anything.

Formally, Arkan didn't come to the prison. It was one of his men. He had a list of prisoners and their dossiers. They had to be the right profile. All he asked was if you were ready to go, to Kosovo... this wasn't a judge's, or a prison warden's decision. It was Arkan's. He is the law in Serbia.

We had 35 guys, prisoners, at one of Arkan's camp for seven days. I can't tell you where. At the camp there was psychological training, target practice. A whole test. Those who failed went back to prison, even though they had the right profile. We had instruction in defensive tactics, offensive tactics.

I was pulled out of prison before the bombardment. Then I went into Kosovo on April 1st. (...)

We headed in new jeeps to Pec. Pec was the center of Kosovo. As soon as we arrived it was pretty heavily damaged. Tougher than we thought...we had a special camp. I can't tell you where it was. Every squad of 15 had a boss. Each unit had a specific task in Kosovo.

We would receive a list of names. Bring this person in alive or dead. I was assigned to arrest people, and had permission to kill them if necessary. (...)

We interacted a lot with certain people at the MUP. There was a kind of crisis council, and some of the information came from there. The lists came from all over, police, city authority, because they had been collecting this kind of information for years. Who were the rich ones, where they lived, who were the important ones, where they lived. (...)

My first operation was to arrest a woman. I had five people with me. We had to shoot her, you can't imagine how she was resisting. How it was. You know, they have these houses with high walls... we had information that she worked for the KLA. We were told to arrest her. So, it was a woman, and with women, you know that they are different. She resisted. We were surprised. You know, a woman—35—who had the gall to resist. So we shot her in the legs. And we handed her over. It wasn't any of my business what happened to her. It's stupid to ask questions beyond my job.

Munja... and others. These were cases of criminals and former police men who were looking for money. These groups had the same directives as we did. Or at least similar. Munja was given names of people, on lists, to liquidate, or arrest, and usually the others were moved out. But Munja's main interest was in robbing people and in raping women. They were a dirty group of men who had no qualms about killing women and children, whether or not they were ordered to do it. They weren't disciplined like us. We carried out orders, and we were not ordered to kill women and children. We killed men, we killed those we were ordered to kill. That's the difference. We were professionals.

Predrag was a policeman in Pec. He joined a special police unit in early 1998. He says he participated in the attack in Cuska on May 14, 1999.

When we got to Cuska I saw that everything had been organized in advance. We weren't supposed to use any heavy weapons because of the threat of NATO attacks. Everything had to be done quietly—Go, finish the job and come back as though nothing had happened. We didn't do the main job—that was the job of other units—but we gave them support.

Everyone had their fixed positions where they were supposed to hold. The Frenkies had its own, the Fog (OPG) had its own, the Yugoslav Army its own... Fog went in first, or as we called them, "the men in black."

The KLA also wore black, so that was one of Fog's advantages against the KLA. They (Fog) went in first, to establish a bridge. We were on the wings... We were on the left side. On the right side was Munja, the Pec boys. That was also a special police unit. It wasn't paramilitary... We made a wedge,

then widened it. Fog usually went with 12 or 24 men. (...)

We had our own lists. And we were interested in men on those lists, men we could get information from. You can assess according to their faces if they had been fighters. If the skin is tanned from the sun, if he's skinny...that would mean he was out fighting. Or if his hands were swollen or dirty.

Miodrag is in his early 20s. He joined the police reservists in Pec in the fall of 1998. He says he participated in the May 14, 1999 attack on Cuska.

We received orders for Cuska the night before the attack. We knew the plan—Munja, the Frenkies, other units... It was a pretty routine operation. The village wasn't defended. Or if the Albanians were defending Cuska it was through bribes. We basically walked in.

In Cuska, I moved on a house with a friend, V. And there we hooked up with another comrade, K.... We broke into the house and there was an old man, an Albanian, inside. He was all alone, smoking a pipe. We started searching the house but V. started up with the old man. The man pretended he didn't speak Serbian. Of course, V. was making fun of the man, threatening him and the guy was completely petrified. V. kept provoking him until the man said, in Serbian, "It's easy for you because you are armed and I am unarmed." So V. took out a knife and threw it to the old man. It hit his shoulder. V. said "now you are equal, now you're armed." And then he just finished the old man off. Shot him in the head.

I know it must sound strange, right now, drinking coffee and listening to the things that happened then. It sounds awful. But you're different then, you enter a different world, a different way of life. You get used to it when there is nonstop killing all around you. One of your guys gets killed, and then it's their people (the Albanians). It's a completely different world, different laws, different morals... Today, I wouldn't even step on an ant. Had anyone asked me (before the war) to kill people I would have said, "no way. Are you crazy? That's only done by..." I'd never do it. But when you enter that realm, I'm telling you, that's the way it is. (...)

[T]he group somehow carries you. Maybe alone you wouldn't do such things. But the group carries you along...

When your country's defense is at stake you can't escape the reality of committing atrocities. Sometimes I can't sleep and I just stare at the ceiling, thinking about these things. The images don't go away. We haven't preserved anything [in Kosovo]. The guys at the top screwed up everything. Serbian politicians screwed us more than the Albanians.

Vaso is in his early 30s. He served in a special Yugoslav Third Army tactical unit. He says he was ordered to take part in the attack on Cuska.

We went there with one aim, to defeat the terrorists. It was out of patriotic reasons I went to fight. And now I ask myself: Should I have been there? Was I delirious? Had I known what I know today, maybe I wouldn't have gone. Again, when you live through difficult trauma, it's hard to figure things out. I walk the streets, alone. I walk all day just thinking. Sometimes I find that I was right to go to fight, other times I feel I was wrong. The pictures from all that are still with me. I still see those innocent people dying. I see a fighter killing a woman in front of her husband and her child. It's something I can never forget.

Kijevë
Kijevo

50

[Our officers] held classes during training and at other times. They would tell us what the Albanians were doing to us, how many people the Albanians had killed. I don't know if it was true but they talked in great detail. They would show us pictures of mutilated bodies and talk about this village or that village where the Serbs were killed or driven out by Albanian terrorists. I don't know if these were true stories but we were blinded by them, by the whole campaign across Serbia. The media was saying the same thing, just one thing. All day, you have one station, one channel, one newscast, one source of information and you have your general, and all of them are talking against the Albanians. You had no chance to like the Albanians, to see them as human beings.

Dragan is in his mid-20s. As a member of a Serbian militia unit calling itself the Czar Dusan brigade, Dragan says he participated in the massacre at Cuska, including the execution of ten Albanian men.

I don't have much contact with my unit. We've scattered. Some have gone abroad, some here, some there... I have difficult nights. I wake up at 4 o'clock in the morning. I can't sleep. So I walk and while I'm walking I ask myself how this all happened, and why. I ask what's going on inside me.

ON METHOD

TEXT AND PHOTOGRAPHS BY
FRED ABRAHAMS

Entering Kosovo in June 1999, after the rampage of Serb and Yugoslav forces and seventy-eight days of NATO bombing, was a shock to my colleagues and me. Burned villages and mass graves littered the landscape.

In the wake of such violence, we debated where the research should begin. Limited resources prohibited an investigation of every case. So we decided to focus on the larger incidents, with an aim to document specific war crimes and to discern a pattern that would shed light on the role of Serbia's political and military elite.

The area of Pec in western Kosovo drew our attention. First, many large-scale killings had been reported there. Second, the region had a large ethnic Serbian population, some of which was active in local security forces. It was possible that witnesses had recognized local men among the perpetrators.

The government of Pec city, run at that time by former members of the Kosovo Liberation Army (KLA), gladly provided general information on war crimes in the area. But the town hall staff possessed material of greater value: photographs of what they claimed were Serbian paramilitaries from Pec and the surrounding villages. KLA fighters had found the photographs after the war, Pec officials said, inside the homes of local Serbs.

The fact that the photos were provided by members of the rebel group, who had an interest in condemning the Serbs, made us wary. As the case evolved, however, independent research proved that the photos indeed depicted individuals who may have been involved in serious crimes.

I scanned the photographs into a laptop computer using a portable scanner/printer. It was not clear at the time how they would be used other than to demonstrate the types of security forces that had apparently been active in the area.

At the same time we began investigating crimes allegedly committed in the nearby village of Cuska, a few kilometers east of Pec. Refugee reports during the NATO bombing had indicated the execution of forty-one men in the village at the hands of Serbian paramilitaries and police. But, because the refugees had been expelled from the village moments before the killings, the reports warranted a closer investigation.

The testimony of survivors and direct witnesses in Cuska confirmed the refugees' stories with stunning accuracy. In one-on-one interviews, the villagers explained how, on May 14, Serbian security forces killed forty-one men in Cuska, as well as twenty-nine others from the nearby villages of Zahac and Pavljan. Miraculously, three men taken away for execution in Cuska had survived the shooting, two of them untouched by bullets.

The survivors and witnesses walked me through the day's events, beginning with the arrival of masked Serbian forces in the early morning. They explained how three groups of men, about ten in each group, were herded into three separate houses, where they were shot and then lit on fire. Two of the survivors took me to the remains of the charred houses where they had been held. They demonstrated how the gunmen had fired upon the men from the doorway with automatic guns. They showed how they hid under the burning bodies and then, when it was safe, slipped out a window and into the hills. Bullet marks pocked one inside wall of each house and bone shards lay among the rubble.

Since Cuska was near some Serbian villages, I decided to show the villagers the scanned photos on the laptop, hoping they might recognize some of the men. I did not expect much. In our experience,

Kosovar Albanians often had difficulty identifying the type of force that had attacked them—Yugoslav Army, Serbian police or paramilitary—let alone specific individuals.

The weather was warm the day I arrived in Cuska with my laptop. Farm animals roamed among the burned-out homes. Most of the villagers had returned only recently and were living in tents provided by the United Nations High Commissioner for Refugees. The laptop contrasted sharply with the scythes used to harvest local crops.

A family that had lost fourteen relatives gathered around the computer. They delegated a young woman, who had had the most contact with the attacking forces, to view the images. She stared intently at the screen, aware that photographs would soon appear but not understanding how.

The first image appeared gradually, moving slowly down the screen. The woman leaned forward, but the sunlight was too strong, and washed out the figures. We retreated to the shade of a nearby barn where it would be easier to view the forms.

The first photograph was of three men looking playful in a large, bare room with windows in the background. The way the men stood, smiling with their arms around each other, made it appear as if they were in a local pub—as if one of the three had just announced his wedding engagement. But the man in the middle wore a green camouflage uniform that belied the illusion of pleasantry. The woman looked intently and shook her head.

The second image appeared on the screen: another group of uniformed men sitting on concrete steps. None of them armed with anything more than a crew cut. Again they appeared calm like a group of teenagers killing time after school. My informant drew in her breath and clicked her tongue which, among Albanians, means "No."

After an uncomfortable wait, a third image appeared. It was a photo of a uniformed man—later identified as Srecko Popovic—standing in front of a burning house with an automatic machine gun in hand. He had short black hair and light stubble. He stared away from the camera to the right, striking a confident, self-conscious, Ramboesque pose.

The woman gasped and lifted her hand to her mouth. With her index finger, she poked at the man's face on the screen, making electronic explosions around his head. "This is the man," she said. "This is the one who came to our house!"

Five other witnesses later placed Srecko Popovic in the village of Cuska on May 14. He and several other local Serbs from the Pec area, I soon learned, belonged to the militia group called Munja (Lightning) that robbed, extorted, raped, and killed ethnic Albanian civilians during the war.

"Do you have family? Do you know what you have done?" said one of the women staring at Popovic's picture. "What kind of heart do you have?"

One by one, the villagers went through the photographs and identified some of the men. Some of the paramilitaries were recognized as having been in Cuska on May 14, although their names were not known. Others were known by name but were not seen in the village on the day of the killing. Most of the paramilitaries were not recognized at all. The villagers appeared to be honest about those they did not know, which gave credibility to their claims.

Over two weeks, dozens of people in Cuska, Zahac, Pavljan, and Pec city gave interviews and viewed the photographs. Whenever possible, one person viewed the pictures at a time. The photographs were mostly shown like a police line-up, one by one, without any comment or suggestion. Working in partnership with two radio journalists from American RadioWorks (who produced an award-winning documentary about Cuska for National Public Radio, on view at www.americanradioworks.org), we were able to paint a picture of the terrible crimes committed in the village, along with portraits of some of the individuals who appear to have committed them.

Even after this laborious process, Human Rights Watch still cannot confirm the authenticity of the photographs. The fact that they were provided by the KLA should heighten suspicion about their origin and accuracy.

Even if the photographs were doctored, however, the villagers positively identified some of the people in the photographs, and it is not possible that this was coordinated between them and the KLA. I asked the KLA for the photographs, rather than receiving them on the KLA's initiative, and I did not mention that they would be shown to villagers in the area.

In the final analysis, all of the allegations of individual responsibility for war crimes were carefully considered before being published. Individuals were only identified by name when at least three separate witnesses had confirmed the name and photo identification. The facts of the case were cross-checked and corroborated through dozens of interviews and all unverifiable claims were discarded.

The methodology employed is another step in the continuing professionalization of human rights research. Using photo identifications, imprecise terms like "Serbian forces" or "armed Albanians" are replaced with the names and faces of individuals accused of committing terrible crimes.

It is unclear whether any of these individuals will be brought to justice because the Kosovo judicial system is in shambles and the International Criminal Tribunal for the former Yugoslavia is, at present, only pursuing the Serbian and Yugoslav leadership. In the larger picture, these men from the Pec area are "small fish."

But identifying them is a helpful first step. Small-time killers might provide information about their commanders. In addition, documenting faces and names helps break the notion of collective guilt: the common perception among Kosovar Albanians that all Serbs are guilty of war crimes, which is not true. With the aid of new technology we have been able, this time, to single out those individuals who should be brought before the international war crimes tribunal and tried for their alleged participation in war crimes.

Pages 206-207 and 211: Villagers identified Serbian security forces on the laptop of a Human Rights Watch researcher.

Pages 212 and 213: Survivors of the massacre in Cuska re-enacted the killing at the crime scene.

Pages 214 and 215: An investigator from the International Criminal Tribunal for the former Yugoslavia examined bullet holes in Cuska.

Pages 216 and 217: Bullet holes circled in white, the burnt floor of a private home and grave markers in western Kosovo, one of them marked "Unidentified."

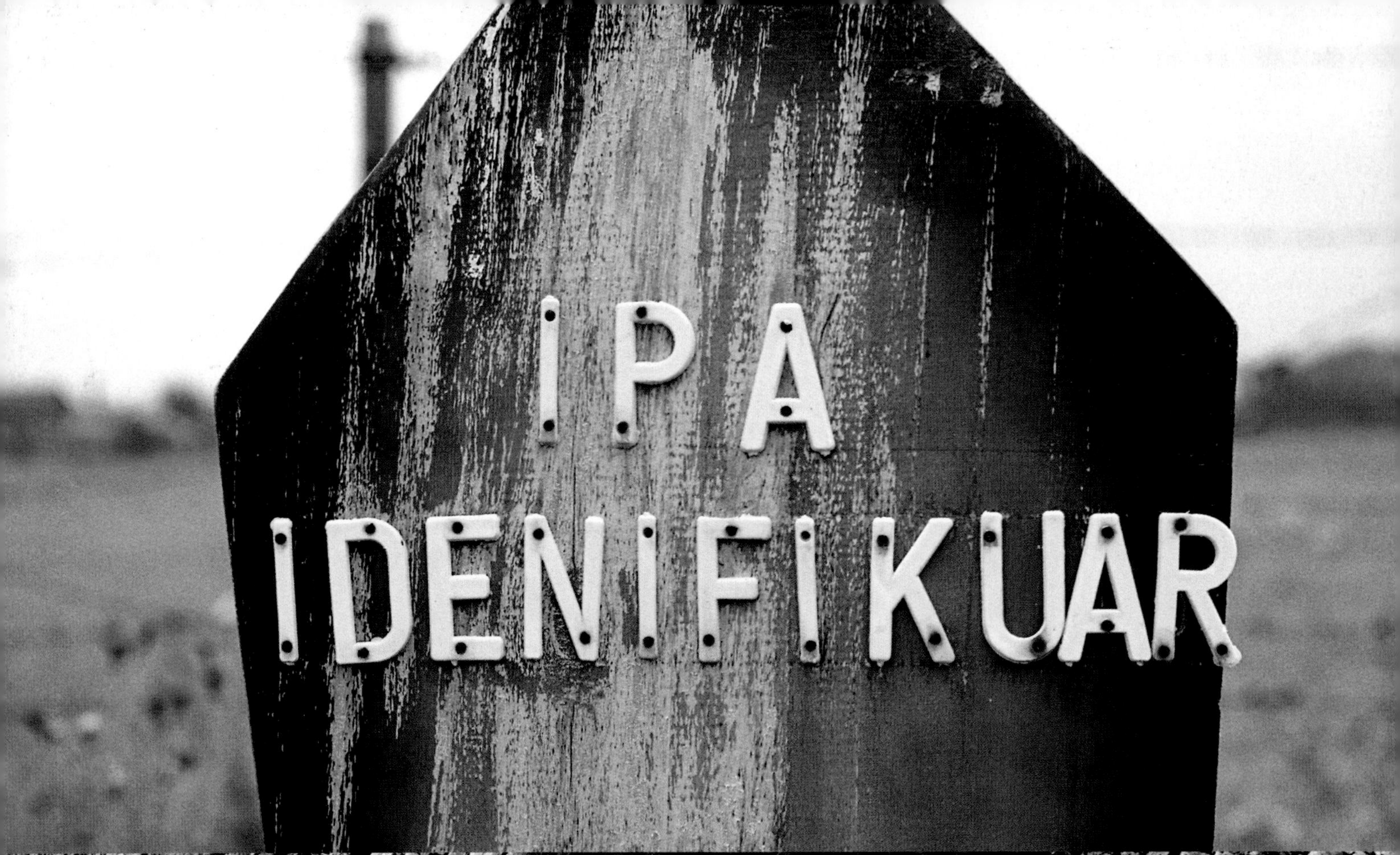
IPA
IDENIFIKUAR
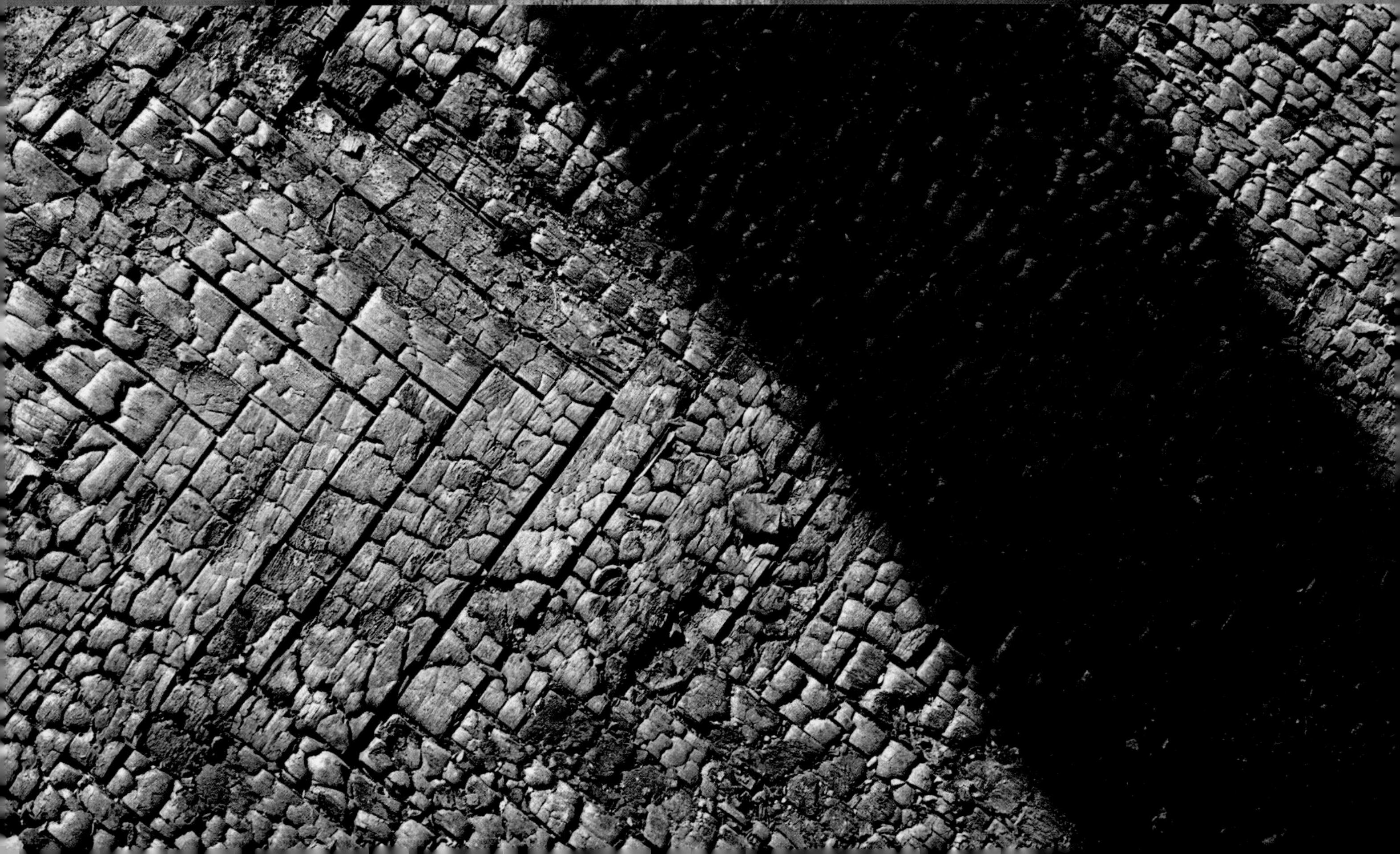

THE VICTIMS

TEXT AND PHOTOGRAPHS BY
FRED ABRAHAMS

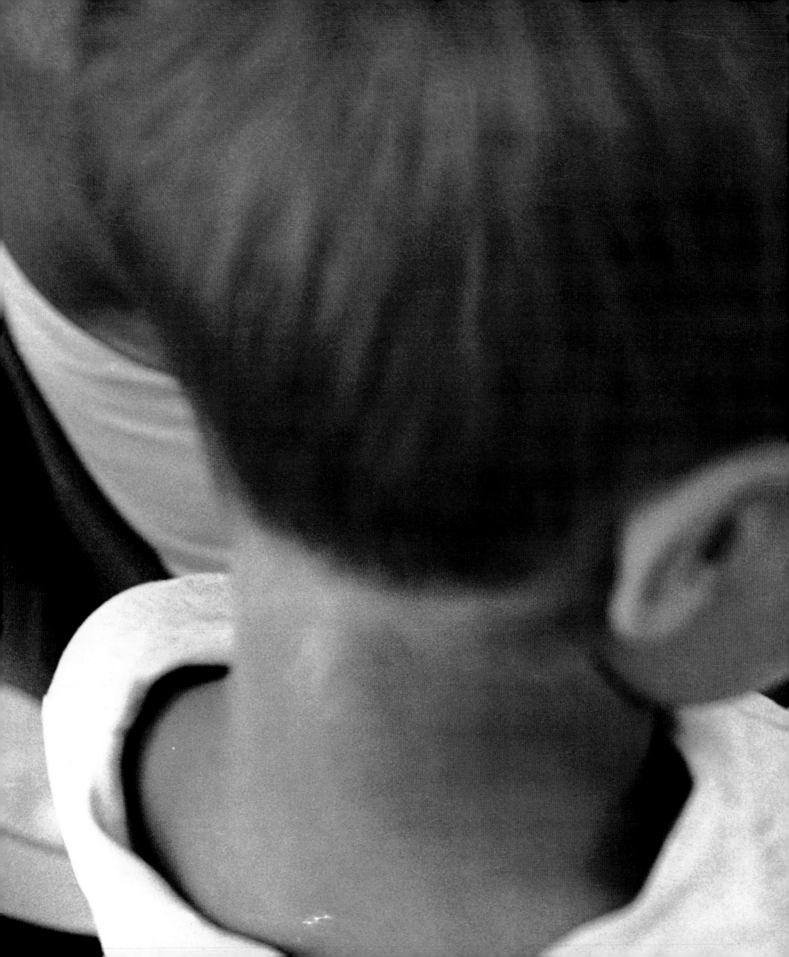

Më 14.05.2000, u bë një v

**NIMON
GASHI**

**MUHARREM
GASHI**

J

IRISH

HALIL

HAR
SHI

AHMET
GASHI

EMIN
GASHI

USA

BRAHIM
GASHI

SKENDER
GASHI

Since the end of the war in Kosovo there have been heated debates about how many Kosovar Albanians were killed in the conflict. NATO and the Kosovo Liberation Army push the numbers up, while the Yugoslav government pushes the numbers down.

The debate is largely irrelevant to the families of Cuska, Zahac, and Pavljan, as well as to hundreds of other families throughout Kosovo—both Albanians and Serbs. For the people who lost friends, neighbors or relatives, postwar propaganda is like a second abuse.

Soon after the massacre in Cuska on May 14, the male villagers who had fled into the hills cautiously returned to gather the bodies. They buried them in a large pit in the village center near the road. By early July 1999, one month after NATO's arrival in Kosovo, wreaths and simple grave markers had been placed on the mound of earth.

Two children who lost their father pinned a handwritten note onto a wooden post next to the common grave:

Daddy,
Don't you know that grandfather Rrustem is coming. He used to see his elder son waiting for him with his car, but now you are under the ground. You don't have the beautiful hands or feet which you had in life.

— Gentiana and Ahmet

One hot day in July the villagers held a formal ceremony with makeshift wooden benches and a stage on the front steps of the village school. Framed photographs of the deceased hung above the speakers who addressed the crowd. Hundreds of mourners sat in rows fanning themselves with newspapers, while local Albanian politicians and KLA commanders, preparing for Kosovo's elections, spoke to the crowd about sacrifice for the nation and independence for Kosovo. A teenage girl in black military uniform read a poem.

Afterwards, a somber procession carried the victims' photographs along a dirt road to the burial spot. A local Imam recited Islamic prayers over the grave as mourners extended their hands forward, palms to the sky.

One year later, the people of Cuska had raised enough money to construct a large marble monument with the names of the massacre victims engraved in neat columns. Like many of the dead across Kosovo, they are now considered martyrs of the nation: those who died so Kosovo could be free, as Kosovo's politicians often say. I wonder whether Gentiana and Ahmet, whose father died in the Cuska massacre, consider their loss in such political terms.

Pages 220-221: A young boy in Pec looks at a photograph of the local militia group known as Munja.

Pages 222 and 223: Family members of the Cuska victims carrying photographs of the deceased in a funeral procession.

Pages 224-225: A one-year memorial to some of the murdered Cuska villagers from the Gashi family. Courtesy of the *Koha Ditore* newspaper.

Pages 226 and 227: Mourners at the July 1999 funeral of the Cuska massacre victims.

Pages 228-229: The marble monument to the Cuska victims erected in the village.

LIST OF THOSE KILLED IN CUSKA ON MAY 14, 1999

1. Muse Gashi, age 64
2. Emin Gashi, age 60
3. Brahim Gashi, age 60
4. Ibish Gashi, age 56
5. Halil Gashi, age 55
6. Syle Gashi, age 49
7. Jashar Gashi, age 47
8. Ahmet Gashi, age 35
9. Skender Gashi, age 37
10. Rame Gashi, age 60
11. Xhafer Gashi, age 42
12. Brahim Gashi, age 56
13. Selim Gashi, age 42
14. Haki Gashi, age 38
15. Iber Kelmendi, age 52
16. Skender Kelmendi, age 46
17. Besim Kelmendi, age 36
18. Erdogan Kelmendi, age 19
19. Brahim Kelmendi, age 40
20. Deme Kelmendi, age 41
21. Mentor Kelmendi, age 23
22. Avdi Berisha, age 64
23. Rasim Rama, age 40
24. Muhamet Shala, age 50
25. Hasan Ceku, age 69
26. Kadri Ceku, age 68
27. Sefedin Lushi, age 41
28. Osman Lushi, age 47
29. Xhafer Lushi, age 46
30. Skender Lushi, age 44
31. Avdulla Lushi, age 60
32. Uke Lushi, age 57
33. Ramiz Lushi, age 41
34. Qaush Lushi, age 51
35. Arian Lushi, age 20
36. Gani Avdylaj, age 42
37. Hasan Avdylaj, age 40
38. Isuf Shala, age 50
39. Emrush Krasniqi, age 49
40. Ismet Dinaj, age 32
41. Zeqir Aliaj, age unknown

LIST OF THOSE KILLED IN PAVLJAN ON MAY 14, 1999

1. Zymber Gashi, age 70
2. Niman Gashi, age 56
3. Shaban Kelmendi, age 52
4. Haxhi Dreshaj, age 41
5. Brahim Nikqi, age 55
6. Hatixhe Nikqi, age 55
7. Alush Selmanaj, age 46
8. Zenun Shala, age unknown
9. Muqe Lulaj, age unknown
10. Xhejrone Nikqi, age unknown

LIST OF THOSE KILLED IN ZAHAC ON MAY 14, 1999

1. Ismet Hyseni, age 41
2. Sabit Hyseni, age 31
3. Naim Hyseni, age 38
4. Agim Hyseni, age 28
5. Bajrush Hyseni, age 24
6. Shpend Hyseni, age 31
7. Shaban Rama, age 45
8. Sadri Rama, age 50
9. Faton Rama, age 24
10. Valdet Rama, age 36
11. Deme Hatashi, age 28
12. Shaban Neziri, age 41
13. Zenel Neziri, age 67
14. Fehmi Gjukiqi, age 23
15. Hysen Gjukiqi, age 21
16. Bekim Delia, age 21
17. Zymber Smajlaj, age 26
18. Shaban Smajlaj, age 23
19. Gezim Cukaj, age 19

CHAIN OF COMMAND

Serbian and Yugoslav Forces in the Conflict

The two principal military forces in Yugoslavia in 1998 and 1999 were the Yugoslav Army (Vojska Jugoslavije, or VJ) and the Serbian Ministry of Internal Affairs (Ministarstvo Unutrasnjih Poslova, or MUP). The police of the Montenegrin Republic remained loyal to the Montenegrin government and were not active in Kosovo.

From the time he became president of Serbia in 1989, Slobodan Milosevic gradually strengthened and expanded the Serbian police over the federal police and the Yugoslav Army, both of which he viewed as less loyal forces. Friction between the Serbian police and Yugoslav Army occasionally emerged over the increased resources and prestige provided to the former.

Only the Serbian regular police, special police, and possibly state security special forces were active in Kosovo in the first half of 1998. The army, although present in the province, was restricted to maintaining security along the borders with Macedonia and Albania. This changed in April 1998, when the army participated in military actions in southwestern Kosovo along the border with Albania. The army and the police cooperated from that point on, but for the most part, actions against the Kosovo Liberation Army (KLA) remained the responsibility of the Serbian Ministry of Internal Affairs throughout 1998.

The primacy of the MUP began to change in late 1998 and early 1999 when President Milosevic reshuffled some key members of the Serbian police and Yugoslav Army, placing known loyalists in top positions. Among other changes, General Dragoljub Ojdanic replaced Momcilo Perisic as General Chief of Staff of the Yugoslav Army and Colonel General Nebojsa Pavkovic was promoted to commander of the VJ's Third Army, which has responsibility for southern Serbia and Kosovo. Radomir Markovic replaced Jovica Stanisic as head of Serbia's security service (secret police). In late March 1999, when faced with attacks by NATO, the police, army, paramilitaries and other irregulars units coordinated their defense against air strikes, attacks on the KLA, and actions against civilians, such as the one in Cuska.

Serbian state security played a major role in Kosovo throughout the 1990s, monitoring Kosovar Albanian political circles, especially the KLA. State security also had a special operations unit called the JSO (Jedinica za Specijalne Operacije, or Special Operations Unit), known informally as "Frenkies Boys," (after the group's supposed founder Frenki Simatovic), which was active in Kosovo in 1998 and 1999 and earlier in Bosnia and Croatia. Commander of the unit was Milorad Lukovic (formerly Milorad Ulemek), who was also known as "Legija."

State security was also involved in organizing and arming the various paramilitary groups active in the former Yugoslavia and Kosovo, including Arkan's Tigers and Seselj's White Eagles. The composition and command structure of the various paramilitary forces and the precise connections they each had to the Serbian and Yugoslav governments remains unclear. But the evidence reveals that they operated in Kosovo with the approval and ongoing political and logistical support of the government, and often in close coordination with regular forces.

Chain of Command

The chain of command for the Yugoslav Army is transparent. As set out here, local commanders in Kosovo reported to the commanders of the Pristina Corps, led by Major General Vladimir Lazarevic. The Pristina Corps reported to the Third Army, commanded by Colonel General Nebojsa Pavkovic, who reported to the General Staff, commanded by General Dragoljub Ojdanic. The overall commander of the VJ was Yugoslav President Slobodan Milosevic, who chaired the Supreme Defense Council.

The structure of the Serbian Ministry of Internal Affairs is more complicated due to the profusion of units and groups within the MUP, such as Munja (Lightning) in Pec. Although these groups were clearly coordinated by the Serbian government under the control of Milosevic, their precise relationship to the government and interior ministry remains unclear. The same is true for the paramilitary forces active in Kosovo, many of whom fought within the official structures of the army or police.

According to the Serbian and Yugoslav constitutions, Yugoslav President Milosevic did not have de jure authority over the Serbian police in a time of peace. Milosevic, however, exercised extensive de facto control over the police and over other institutions nominally under the competence of Serbia. In addition, under the Yugoslav Law on Defense, during a state of war, the Serbian and federal police come under the command of the Yugoslav Army. A state of war was declared in Yugoslavia on March 24, 1999, which gave Slobodan Milosevic, as supreme commander of the army, both de jure and de facto control of the police.

The MUP's de jure structure does not necessarily reflect the de facto reality. The role of Serbia's Minister of Internal Affairs, Vlajko Stojiljkovic, for instance, is considered by Serbian and foreign observers of the Serbian security structures to have been subordinate to that of President Milosevic and perhaps also to Yugoslav Deputy Prime Minister Nikola Sainovic, widely considered Milosevic's point-man on Kosovo. Various lines of command and control within and between state security, public security, the paramilitary forces, and the president are still unknown. Lastly, the methods and structure of cooperation between the MUP and VJ remain unclear.

Command Responsibility

The case against the Serbian and Yugoslav leadership is convincing. According to Article 7 of the statute of the International Criminal Tribunal for the former Yugoslavia (ICTY), the direct perpetrator of a crime, as well as the military or political leaders who ordered that crime, can be prosecuted. Paragraph three adds that a superior is accountable for crimes committed if he or she knew or had reason to know about such acts and failed to take steps to prevent them or to punish the perpetrators.

The extent and systematic nature of the crimes in Kosovo make it highly implausible that the Serbian and Yugoslav leadership did not know that crimes were being committed. Numerous statements by the Serbian and Yugoslav government or military demonstrate that the top leadership was regularly apprised of the security situation in Kosovo. Well distributed reports by the media and nongovernmental organizations, such as Human Rights Watch, Amnesty International, and the Humanitarian Law Center, repeatedly documented abuses by Serbian and Yugoslav forces.

Despite this, there is no evidence to suggest serious attempts by the Milosevic government to hinder government or paramilitary operations, despite repeated and credible reports that they had committed atrocities. Rather than being held accountable, hundreds of army and police personnel were promoted or given awards after the war, such as the Order of the National Hero and Order of the Yugoslav Flag, including most of the top military and police leadership.

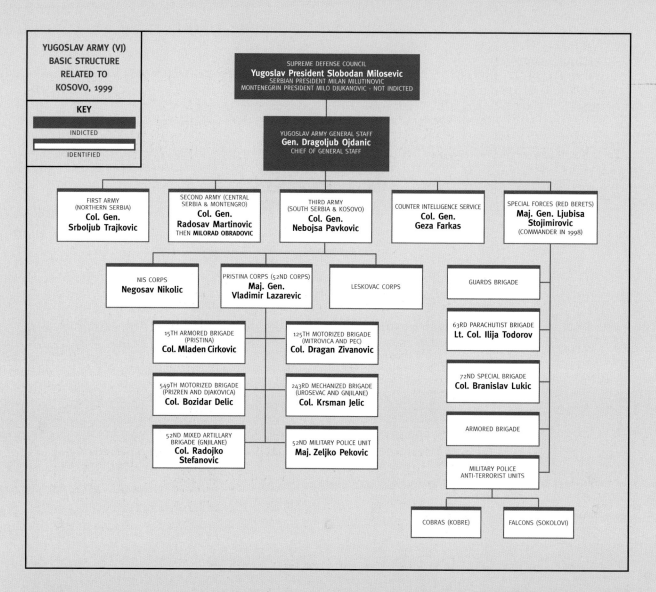

YUGOSLAV ARMY (VJ) BASIC STRUCTURE RELATED TO KOSOVO, 1999

KEY

INDICTED

IDENTIFIED

SUPREME DEFENSE COUNCIL
Yugoslav President Slobodan Milosevic
SERBIAN PRESIDENT MILAN MILUTINOVIC
MONTENEGRIN PRESIDENT MILO DJUKANOVIC - NOT INDICTED

YUGOSLAV ARMY GENERAL STAFF
Gen. Dragoljub Ojdanic
CHIEF OF GENERAL STAFF

FIRST ARMY (NORTHERN SERBIA)
Col. Gen. Srboljub Trajkovic

SECOND ARMY (CENTRAL SERBIA & MONTENEGRO)
Col. Gen. Radosav Martinovic
THEN **MILORAD OBRADOVIC**

THIRD ARMY (SOUTH SERBIA & KOSOVO)
Col. Gen. Nebojsa Pavkovic

COUNTER INTELLIGENCE SERVICE
Col. Gen. Geza Farkas

SPECIAL FORCES (RED BERETS)
Maj. Gen. Ljubisa Stojimirovic
(COMMANDER IN 1998)

NIS CORPS
Negosav Nikolic

PRISTINA CORPS (52ND CORPS)
Maj. Gen. Vladimir Lazarevic

LESKOVAC CORPS

GUARDS BRIGADE

15TH ARMORED BRIGADE (PRISTINA)
Col. Mladen Cirkovic

125TH MOTORIZED BRIGADE (MITROVICA AND PEC)
Col. Dragan Zivanovic

63RD PARACHUTIST BRIGADE
Lt. Col. Ilija Todorov

549TH MOTORIZED BRIGADE (PRIZREN AND DJAKOVICA)
Col. Bozidar Delic

243RD MECHANIZED BRIGADE (UROSEVAC AND GNJILANE)
Col. Krsman Jelic

72ND SPECIAL BRIGADE
Col. Branislav Lukic

52ND MIXED ARTILLARY BRIGADE (GNJILANE)
Col. Radojko Stefanovic

52ND MILITARY POLICE UNIT
Maj. Zeljko Pekovic

ARMORED BRIGADE

MILITARY POLICE ANTI-TERRORIST UNITS

COBRAS (KOBRE)

FALCONS (SOKOLOVI)

On May 24, 1999, citing war crimes committed in Kosovo, the ICTY indicted Slobodan Milosevic and four other Serbian or Yugoslav officials: Serbian President Milan Milutinovic, Yugoslav Deputy Prime Minister Nikola Sainovic, Serbian Minister of Internal Affairs Vlajko Stojiljkovic, and Yugoslav Army General Chief of Staff General Dragoljub Ojdanic. The Kosovo Liberation Army was also under investigation for war crimes committed against Serbs, Roma and other non ethnic-Albanians, as well as against Kosovar Albanians considered "collaborators" with the Serbian state.

The new Serbian and Yugoslav governments took some steps toward accountability after the fall of Milosevic in October 2000. On April 1, 2001, Milosevic was arrested on charges of corruption. On June 28, he was transferred to the ICTY to face charges of war crimes. In May 2001, a Yugoslav Army military court charged 193 VJ soldiers and reservists with criminal offenses against the life and property of the Albanian community in Kosovo, although details of the charges remained unclear.

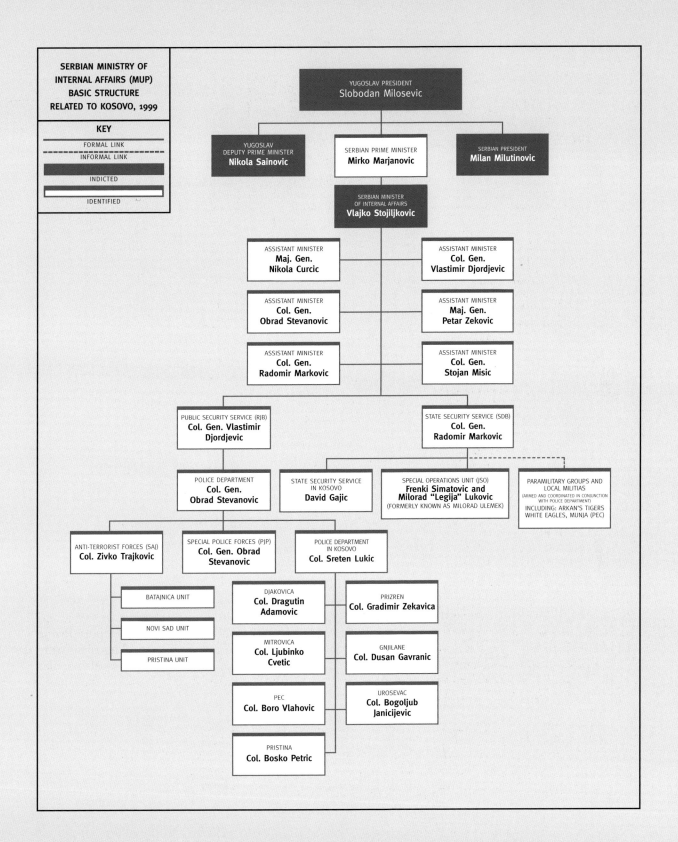

SERBIAN MINISTRY OF INTERNAL AFFAIRS (MUP) BASIC STRUCTURE RELATED TO KOSOVO, 1999

KEY

FORMAL LINK
INFORMAL LINK
INDICTED
IDENTIFIED

YUGOSLAV PRESIDENT
Slobodan Milosevic

YUGOSLAV DEPUTY PRIME MINISTER
Nikola Sainovic

SERBIAN PRIME MINISTER
Mirko Marjanovic

SERBIAN PRESIDENT
Milan Milutinovic

SERBIAN MINISTER OF INTERNAL AFFAIRS
Vlajko Stojiljkovic

ASSISTANT MINISTER
Maj. Gen. Nikola Curcic

ASSISTANT MINISTER
Col. Gen. Vlastimir Djordjevic

ASSISTANT MINISTER
Col. Gen. Obrad Stevanovic

ASSISTANT MINISTER
Maj. Gen. Petar Zekovic

ASSISTANT MINISTER
Col. Gen. Radomir Markovic

ASSISTANT MINISTER
Col. Gen. Stojan Misic

PUBLIC SECURITY SERVICE (RJB)
Col. Gen. Vlastimir Djordjevic

STATE SECURITY SERVICE (SDB)
Col. Gen. Radomir Markovic

POLICE DEPARTMENT
Col. Gen. Obrad Stevanovic

STATE SECURITY SERVICE IN KOSOVO
David Gajic

SPECIAL OPERATIONS UNIT (JSO)
Frenki Simatovic and Milorad "Legija" Lukovic
(FORMERLY KNOWN AS MILORAD ULEMEK)

PARAMILITARY GROUPS AND LOCAL MILITIAS
(ARMED AND COORDINATED IN CONJUNCTION WITH POLICE DEPARTMENT)
INCLUDING: ARKAN'S TIGERS WHITE EAGLES, MUNJA (PEC)

ANTI-TERRORIST FORCES (SAJ)
Col. Zivko Trajkovic

SPECIAL POLICE FORCES (PJP)
Col. Gen. Obrad Stevanovic

POLICE DEPARTMENT IN KOSOVO
Col. Sreten Lukic

BATAJNICA UNIT

NOVI SAD UNIT

PRISTINA UNIT

DJAKOVICA
Col. Dragutin Adamovic

PRIZREN
Col. Gradimir Zekavica

MITROVICA
Col. Ljubinko Cvetic

GNJILANE
Col. Dusan Gavranic

PEC
Col. Boro Vlahovic

UROSEVAC
Col. Bogoljub Janicijevic

PRISTINA
Col. Bosko Petric

233

CHRONOLOGY

1989-90   Amidst rising nationalism in Serbia, Kosovo's constitutional status as an autonomous province is revoked. Tens of thousands of ethnic Albanians in Kosovo, who make up 90 percent of the population, lose their jobs. Special police forces begin a decade of repression.

1991   In a secret referendum, Kosovar Albanians vote for a Republic of Kosovo independent of Yugoslavia.

1991-92   The Socialist Federal Republic of Yugoslavia begins to disintegrate. Wars begin in the former republics of Slovenia, Croatia, and Bosnia-Herzegovina. The international community imposes sanctions on Yugoslavia. The Kosovar Albanians begin nonviolent resistance to Belgrade's oppressive rule.

1993   The United Nations Security Council establishes the International Criminal Tribunal for the former Yugoslavia, based in The Hague.

1995   The Dayton Accords end the war in Bosnia, but Kosovo is not on the agenda.

1996   The Kosovo Liberation Army (KLA) begins more coordinated attacks against Serbian police in Kosovo.

1997   In October, Serbian police break up Kosovar Albanian student demonstrations demanding better Albanian-language education. The KLA increases its attacks against the police. Opposition rallies and student demonstrations in Serbia protest electoral fraud by President Slobodan Milosevic in late 1997 and early 1998.

1998
February/March   Serbian forces attack the neighboring villages of Likosane (Likoshane) and Cirez (Qirez) in Kosovo's Drenica region, killing twenty-five ethnic Albanians. Shortly thereafter, special police attack the family compound of Adem Jashari, a local KLA leader, in Donji Prekaz (Prekaz e Ulet), killing an estimated fifty-eight members of the family. The attacks mobilize the ethnic Albanian community and swell the ranks of the KLA. On March 31, the UN Security Council adopts Resolution 1160 condemning the excessive use of force by the Serbian police force against civilians in Kosovo and establishes an arms embargo against Yugoslavia.

Mid-May   Serbian and Yugoslav forces launch an offensive in western Kosovo along the border with Albania, apparently intended to sever supply routes of the KLA. Approximately 45,000 ethnic Albanians flee into Albania or Montenegro, sometimes under fire from the police and army. Government forces burn most villages in the region.

July   The KLA mounts its first major offensive, an attack on the town of Orahovac (Rrahovec). Approximately forty Serbs go missing and at least forty-two ethnic Albanians are killed when the police retake the town after two days. The government begins a summer-long anti-insurgency campaign that leaves hundreds dead and more than 200,000 internally displaced.

September	Serbian forces kill twenty-one members of the Deliaj family, mostly women and children, in Gornje Obrinje (Abri e Eperme). In nearby Golubovac (Golubofc), thirteen men are executed.
October	Milosevic agrees to a cease-fire and the deployment of a monitoring mission run by OSCE—the Kosovo Verification Mission.
1999 January 15	Serbian forces kill forty-five ethnic Albanians in Racak, prompting international outcry and calls for a more forceful international response.
February 6	Talks with Kosovar Albanians, the Serbian government, and the international community begin in Rambouillet, France. After a break in the talks, the Albanians sign the agreement but the Serbian delegation refuses.
March 19	The Kosovo Verification Mission withdraws from Kosovo. The next day, Serbian and Yugoslav armed units launch an offensive in parts of Kosovo, driving thousands of ethnic Albanians out of their homes.
March 24	NATO begins bombing Yugoslavia. The Serbian and Yugoslav government offensive escalates dramatically. Over the next eleven weeks, more than 800,000 Kosovar Albanians are forcibly expelled. As many as 10,000 are killed.
May 14	Seventy Kosovar Albanian villagers in Cuska, Pavljan, and Zahac, east of Pec, are murdered in early morning raids.
May 27	Slobodan Milosevic and four other Serbian and Yugoslav leaders are indicted by the UN war crimes tribunal for crimes against humanity committed in Kosovo.
June 9	NATO and Yugoslav forces sign the Military Technical Agreement to stop the bombing and allow for the deployment of NATO troops in Kosovo.
June 10	The UN Security Council adopts Resolution 1244 on Kosovo which mandates a UN administration in the province. Kosovo is to remain a part of Yugoslavia.
July 23	Unidentified individuals murder fourteen Serbian farmers near the Kosovo village of Gracko in the largest single killing of Kosovo's minorities since the entry of NATO. Throughout 1999, 2000 and 2001, Serbs, Roma, Bosniaks and other non-ethnic Albanians are harassed, attacked or killed, forcing the departure from the province of at least 150,000 people. Minorities who remain in Kosovo are forced to live in mono-ethnic enclaves with around-the-clock NATO protection.

GLOSSARY OF TERMS

For more information, see Roy Gutman and David Rieff (eds.), *Crimes of War: What the Public Should Know* (New York: W.W. Norton, 1999) [www.crimesofwar.org]; and W. Michael Reisman and Chris T. Antoniou (eds.), *The Laws of War: A Comprehensive Collection of Primary Documents on International Laws Governing Armed Conflict* (New York: Vintage Books, 1994).

Command Responsibility

Establishing command responsibility will be key to the prosecution's case against Slobodan Milosevic and his four co-defendants before the International Criminal Tribunal for the former Yugoslavia who face charges of crimes against humanity and war crimes. Article 86 of Additional Protocol I to the 1949 Geneva Conventions states: "the fact that a breach of the Conventions or of this Protocol was committed by a subordinate does not absolve his superiors from penal disciplinary responsibility as the case may be if they knew, or had information which would have enabled them to conclude in the circumstances at the time that he was committing or was going to commit such a breach and if they did not take all feasible measures within their powers to prevent or repress the breach."

Command responsibility extends to officers in the chain of command who know or have reason to know that their subordinates are committing war crimes and who fail to act to stop them. Under the 1998 statue of the new International Criminal Court, military commanders are liable for crimes that they "knew or should have known" about under circumstances at the time, and only for those crimes committed by forces under their "effective command and control." Military commanders are liable if they "failed to take all necessary and reasonable measures" to prevent and repress such crimes that subordinates "were committing or about to commit" or if they failed to report such crimes to proper authorities.

Crimes against Humanity

Next to genocide, crimes against humanity—a term which originated in the 1907 Hague Convention preamble—is the most serious state crime that can be committed against a civilian population. It is defined in eleven international texts, including the statutes of the International Criminal Tribunal for the former Yugoslavia (ICTY), the International Criminal Tribunal for Rwanda (ICTR), and the International Criminal Court (ICC). In 1945, the Allies developed the Agreement for the Prosecution and Punishment of the Major War Criminals of the European Axis and Charter of the International Military Tribunal, sitting at Nuremberg, which contained the following definition of crimes against humanity:

> Crimes against humanity: murder, extermination, enslavement, deportation, and other inhumane acts committed against civilian populations, before or during the war; or persecutions on political, racial or religious grounds in execution or in connection with any crime within the jurisdiction of the Tribunal, whether or not in violation of the domestic law of the country where perpetrated.

The ICTY and ICTR statutes added rape and torture to the list of crimes against humanity. The ICC statute expanded it to include the crimes of enforced disappearances of persons and apartheid. To some extent, crimes against humanity overlap with genocide and war crimes. But crimes against humanity are distinguishable from genocide in that they do not require an intent to "destroy in whole or part" but only to target a given group and carry out a policy of "widespread or systematic" violations. Crimes against humanity are also distinguishable from war crimes in that they apply in time of both war and peace.

Crimes against humanity are a nonderogable rule of international law. The implication is that they are subject to universal jurisdiction, meaning that all states can exercise their jurisdiction in prosecuting a perpetrator irrespective of where the crime was committed.

Ethnic Cleansing

Ethnic cleansing—the use of force or intimidation to remove people of a certain ethnic or religious group from an area—is a blanket term; no specific crime goes by that name but in practice, the term covers a wide variety of criminal offenses. The UN Commission of Experts, in a January 1993 report, defined "ethnic cleansing" as "rendering an area ethnically homogenous by using force or intimidation to remove persons of given groups from the area." It said ethnic cleansing was carried out in the former Yugoslavia by means of murder, torture, arbitrary arrest and detention, extrajudicial executions, rape and sexual assault, confinement of the civilian population, deliberate military attacks or threats of attacks on civilians and civilian areas, and wanton destruction of property. The Commission's final report in May 1994 added these crimes: mass murder, mistreatment of civilian prisoners and prisoners of war, use of civilians as human shields, destruction of cultural property, robbery of personal property, and attacks on hospitals, medical personnel, and locations with the Red Cross/Red Crescent emblem.

Article 49 of the Fourth Geneva Convention of 1949 forbids "individual or mass forcible transfers, as well as deportation of protected persons from occupied territory to the territory of the Occupying Power or to that of any other country." It adds that only the security of the civilian population or "imperative military reasons" may justify evacuation of civilians in occupied territory.

Extrajudicial Execution

Both international humanitarian law and human rights law state that it is illegal to execute an accused person without first giving him or her a fair trial. Under international humanitarian law, extrajudicial execution is usually termed "willful killing without judicial process." If the victims are enemy prisoners of war (including accredited journalists and civilian suppliers and contractors attached to enemy armed forces), or medical or religious personnel attached to the armed services, such executions are grave breaches under the Third Geneva Convention. If they are enemy civilians, their execution is a grave breach of the Fourth Geneva Convention.

FRY (Federal Republic of Yugoslavia)

FRY was officially established in April 1992 after the break-up of the former Yugoslavia, which was known as the Socialist Federal Republic of Yugoslavia (SFRY). FRY is comprised of two constituent republics, Serbia and Montenegro, with its capitol in Belgrade. Kosovo was an autonomous province of Serbia until 1989 when the Serbian government revoked that status. As of September 2001, Kosovo remained a part of Serbia, although under the administration of the United Nations pursuant to UN Resolution 1244.

Genocide

Article II of the Convention on the Prevention and Punishment of the Crime of Genocide, adopted by the UN General Assembly on December 9, 1948, defines genocide as meaning:

> [A]ny of the following acts committed with intent to destroy, in whole or in part, a national, ethnic, racial, or religious group as such: (a) Killing members of the group; (b) Causing serious bodily or mental harm to members of the group; (c) Deliberately inflicting on the group conditions of life calculated to bring about its physical destruction in whole or part; (d) Imposing measures intending to prevent births within the group; (e) Forcibly transferring children of the group to another group.

Article II of the Convention states: "The following acts shall be punishable: (a) Genocide; (b) Conspiracy to commit genocide; (c) Direct and public incitement to commit genocide; (d) Attempt to commit genocide; (e) Complicity in genocide. Article IV specifies that "Persons committing genocide or any of the other acts enumerated in Article III shall be punished, whether they are constitutionally responsible rulers, public officials or private individuals."

Hague Conventions

Many of the laws dealing explicitly with conduct in the course of armed conflict were initially codified at conferences in The Hague, Netherlands at the beginning of the twentieth century. Among the laws, rules, and duties codified by the Hague Conventions of 1899 and 1907—often referred to as "Hague Law"--are policies about war on land, cessation of hostilities, occupation of territory, qualifications of belligerents, prisoners of war, the status of merchant ships during war, the laying of automatic submarine contact mines, bombardment by naval forces, and the rights and duties of neutral powers. Further conventions deal with the rules of aerial warfare (1923); protection of cultural property (1954); and suppression of unlawful seizure of aircraft (1970).

Indiscriminate Attack

An indiscriminate attack is one in which the attacker does not take measures to avoid hitting nonmilitary objectives, that is, civilians and civilian objects. It also includes using means and methods that cannot be directed at specific military objectives or whose effects cannot be limited. The 1977 Additional Protocol I to the Geneva Conventions of 1949 specifies: "Parties to the conflict shall at all times distinguish between the civilian population and combatants and between civilian objects and military objectives and accordingly shall direct their operations against military objectives."

Protocol I defines military objectives as limited to "those objects which by their nature, location, purpose or use make an effective contribution to military action and whose total or partial destruction, capture or neutralization, in the circumstances ruling at the time, offers a definite military advantage." If the harm to civilians is proportionate to the military advantage expected, the attack, other things being equal, is a legal act of war. If the harm is "exclusive in relation to the concrete and direct military advantage anticipated," the attack is prohibited, whether or not indiscriminate.

Internally Displaced Persons

Internally displaced persons, or IDPs, have been forced to flee their homes, or places of habitual residence, as a result of armed conflict, situations of generalized violence, violations of human rights, or natural or human-made disasters, and have not crossed an internationally recognized border. If such persons were to be sent across an international border, they would be considered refugees.

Article 49 of the Fourth Geneva Convention provides that "individual or mass forcible transfers…
are prohibited, regardless of their motive." Additional Protocol II of 1977, which applies in internal
conflicts, provides that forced civilian displacement may be undertaken legally only when civilians'
very safety or "imperative military reasons" require it. The International Committee of the Red
Cross Commentary to the Additional Protocols states that the intent here is to minimize civilian
displacement that is politically motivated.

International Criminal Tribunal for the former Yugoslavia (ICTY)

ICTY was established by the UN Security Council on May 25,1993, to prosecute and try persons
allegedly responsible for serious violations of international humanitarian law committed in the
territory of the former Yugoslavia since 1991. Based in The Hague, Netherlands, ICTY has the
power to prosecute persons committing or ordering to be committed genocide, crimes against
humanity, grave breaches of the 1949 Geneva Conventions, or the laws or customs of war.

International Humanitarian Law

The genesis of international humanitarian law, often referred to as "Geneva Law," dates back to the
establishment of the International Committee of the Red Cross (ICRC) in Geneva in 1864 by Henry
Dunant, a Geneva banker who had witnessed the massive horrors of the Battle of Solferino in
northern Italy in 1859. The ICRC, which concerns itself with reinforcing and extending
humanitarian aspects of the laws of war and, in particular, securing the protection of prisoners of war
and other noncombatants, has convened many of its conferences in Geneva where it maintains its
headquarters. Since 1977, the ICRC has sought to merge "Geneva Law" and "Hague Law" into a
single comprehensive body of what it would like to be known as "humanitarian law" (see Hague
Conventions).

Kosovo Liberation Army (KLA)

Known in Albanian as the Ushtria Clirimtare e Kosoves (UCK), the KLA began to take form in the
mid-1990s as a disorganized group of rebels who advocated violent means to achieve independence
for Kosovo. The group swelled in size in fall 1998, after Serbian security forces killed dozens of
ethnic Albanian civilians in an attack on a KLA stronghold. The group continued to wage a guerrilla
war against Serbian and Yugoslav forces throughout 1998 and 1999. It was also responsible for
violations of international humanitarian law, such as executions of civilians, abductions, and sexual
assault. Kosovo Serbs as well as Albanians considered collaborators with the Serbian government
were threatened, attacked, and killed. For more information, see two Human Rights Watch reports:
Abuses Against Serbs and Roma in the New Kosovo (August 1999) and Humanitarian Law Violations
in Kosovo (October 1998).

MUP (Ministarstvo Unutrasnjih Poslova) —Serbian Ministry of Internal Affairs

The MUP is the main security force of the Republic of Serbia, one of the two republics in the Federal
Republic of Yugoslavia (FRY). The MUP is primarily comprised of a public security service (police,
special police, anti-terrorist forces) and a state security service (secret police and a special operations
unit). Together with the Yugoslav Army, the MUP was active in Kosovo during 1998 and 1999. The
Minister of Internal Affairs at the time was Vlajko Stojiljkovic, although ultimate authority rested
with then Yugoslav president Slobodan Milosevic.

North Atlantic Treaty Organization (NATO)

Established in 1949, NATO is a trans-Atlantic security alliance that primarily links the United States
to the countries of Western Europe. Initially intended as a military alliance during the Cold War,

NATO has become increasingly involved in internal conflicts, such as in the former Yugoslavia. In March 1999, NATO began a 78-day bombing campaign over Yugoslavia that resulted in the withdrawal of Serbian and Yugoslav forces from the province. During the bombing, NATO was responsible for some violations of international humanitarian law: specifically, failing to adequately minimize civilian casualties and using cluster bombs near populated areas. For more information, see two Human Rights Watch reports: *Civilian Deaths in the NATO Air Campaign* (February 2000) and *Ticking Time Bombs: NATO's Use of Cluster Munitions in Yugoslavia* (June 1999).

Organization for Security and Cooperation in Europe (OSCE)

The OSCE is a regional security organization with 55 participating states from Europe, Central Asia, and North America. The OSCE is primarily an instrument for early warning, conflict prevention, crisis management, and post-conflict rehabilitation. It addresses a wide range of security-related issues including arms control, preventive diplomacy, confidence- and security-building measures, human rights, election monitoring, and economic and environmental security. Its decisions are politically but not legally binding.

From October 1998 to March 1999, the OSCE had a monitoring mission in Kosovo called the Kosovo Verification Mission (KVM). The organization withdrew from Kosovo during the NATO bombing of Yugoslavia but was based in neighboring Albania and Macedonia, where field workers interviewed Kosovar Albanian refugees. The OSCE resumed operation in Kosovo in June 1999. In December 1999, the OSCE released two voluminous reports on violations of human rights in Kosovo, one dealing with events between March and June 1999, and the other documenting human rights abuses after the war (see *Kosovo/Kosova: As Seen, As Told, Parts I and II*, available at www.osce.org/kosovo/reports/hr/part1/.

Paramilitary

For much of the past century, the term "paramilitary" applied to forces that were typically uniformed, subjected to a formal hierarchy and disciplinary norms like that of the military, and armed with light military weapons. The Carabineros of Chile, the Civil Guard of Peru, and the National Guard of El Salvador are paramilitary in this sense. In the 1960s, however, the common usage of the term was sometimes inverted. From applying strictly to highly regulated, uniformed, military-like forces, "paramilitary" came to apply to forces that were irregular: often covert, operating in plain clothes, absent the rigid norms, requirements, and traditions of a military institution, and sharing an unconventional military mission. This usage was a feature of the United States' military doctrine of unconventional warfare and counterinsurgency after 1961 and was reflected in the training and doctrine of Latin American and other allied armies from that time. "Paramilitary" became the term of art for armed government-sponsored organizations which had little in common with conventional military institutions and whose official status was sometimes left deliberately ambiguous.

The term has been used by the media, by government organs, and in popular speech to apply to forces seen as partners of the state's security services in combating subversion and armed opposition groups, even when these official bodies deny any collaboration with them. The term "paramilitary" has also come to apply to the methodology employed by covert units of the regular security services of many countries. When irregular and often illegal operations are carried out by military or military-like units, these operations—and the units themselves—units are characterized as "paramilitary" to distinguish them from conventional forces and operations.

Prisoners of War

Prisoners of war are combatants who have surrendered or, due to injury, are unable to continue to fight and so come into the control of their adversary. Since earlier conventions dealing with prisoners of war proved inadequate, the drafters of the Geneva Conventions of 1949 aspired to establish a detailed, humane regime governing the treatment of combatants who have been captured by their adversaries. The 1977 Protocol I to the Geneva Conventions of 1949 expanded the categories of individuals that may be considered combatants and thus entitled to the protections of the 1949 Conventions. Protocol I includes as combatants those individuals who do not wear uniforms to distinguish themselves as combatants, on the condition that they carry their arms openly during each military engagement and are visible to the adversary while they are engaged in a military deployment.

Rape as a War Crime

Rape and other forms of sexual violence, including sexual abuse, sexual slavery, and forced prostitution, are fundamental assaults on human health, physical and mental integrity, and dignity. In the context of an international armed conflict, they therefore qualify as grave breaches under the 1949 Geneva Conventions and Additional Protocol I of 1977. The Conventions explicitly require nations to prosecute persons who commit acts such as "torture or inhuman treatment" and "willfully caus[e] great suffering or serious injury to body or health" against any person. The Fourth Geneva Convention provides that women must be protected against "rape, enforced prostitution, or any form of indecent assault." Similarly, Protocol II to the Geneva Conventions of 1949, which governs the protection of civilians in internal armed conflicts, explicitly outlaws "outrages upon personal dignity, in particular humiliating and degrading treatment, rape, forced prostitution and any form of indecent assault."

- Both the International Criminal Tribunal for the former Yugoslavia (ICTY) and the International Criminal Tribunal for Rwanda (ICTR) are empowered to prosecute rape and other forms of sexual violence as genocide, crimes against humanity, and war crimes.

- In September 1998, the ICTR handed down the first international conviction of genocide and crimes against humanity based on rape. The landmark decision went against Jean-Paul Akayesu, who served as mayor of the Taba commune and was responsible for maintaining law and public order. He was accused of allowing police under his authority to rape and torture mostly Tutsi women who had sought his protection. Akayesu was sentenced to life imprisonment.

- In December 1998, the ICTY found Anto Furundzija guilty as a co-perpetrator of torture for raping and sexually assaulting a woman while he served as the local commander of the Croatian Defense Council military police. The Court held that under certain circumstances, rape and other serious sexual assaults may constitute torture under international law.

- In February 2001, the ICTY issued a verdict declaring that rape and sexual enslavement constitute crimes against humanity. Three Bosnian Serb men were found guilty of rape of Bosnian Muslim women and girls—some as young as 12 and 15 years of age—in Foca, eastern Bosnia-Herzegovina. Two of the accused were also found guilty of sexual enslavement as a crime against humanity by holding women and girls captive in several de facto detention centers near Foca.

Finally, the statute of the International Criminal Court includes "rape, sexual slavery, enforced prostitution, forced pregnancy, enforced sterilization, or any other form of sexual violence of comparable gravity" in its definition of crimes against humanity.

Refugees

Refugees are persons who are outside of their country of origin and are unable, or unwilling, to avail themselves of the protection of their country due to a well-founded fear of persecution based on their race, religion, nationality, membership of a particular social group, or political opinion. The 1951 UN Convention Relating to the Status of Refugees defines who refugees are and how they are to be treated. This convention endeavors to assure refugees the widest possible exercise of their fundamental rights and freedoms. Most importantly, no country may expel or return ("refoul") refugees to the frontiers of territories where their life or freedom would be threatened on account of their race, religion, nationality, membership in a particular social group, or political opinion.

United Nations High Commissioner for Refugees (UNHCR)

UNHCR is mandated by the United Nations to lead and coordinate international action for the world-wide protection of refugees and the resolution of refugee problems. UNHCR's primary purpose is to safeguard the rights and well-being of refugees. During the NATO bombing of Kosovo in 1999, UNHCR helped accommodate more than 800,000 Kosovar Albanian refugees.

VJ (Vojska Jugoslavije) — Yugoslav Army

The VJ is the army of the Federal Republic of Yugoslavia, although it is dominated by political and military leaders in Serbia. The VJ is comprised of three armies, the third of which is responsible for Kosovo. During 1998 and 1999, the head of the Third Army was Col. Gen. Nebojsa Pavkovic. He reported to Army Gen. Dragoljub Ojdanic, who was Chief of the Army General Staff. Ojdanic reported to Yugoslavia's Supreme Defense Council, which was headed by the country's supreme commander, Yugoslav President Slobodan Milosevic.

War Crimes

War crimes are those violations of the laws of war—or international humanitarian law—that incur individual criminal responsibility. The 1949 Geneva Conventions marked the first inclusion in a humanitarian law treaty of a set of war crimes known as the grave breaches of the conventions. Each of the four Geneva Conventions (on wounded and sick on land, wounded and sick at sea, prisoners of war, and civilians) contains its own list of grave breaches. As noted in *Crimes of War: What the Public Should Know* (p. 374), the list in its totality consists of:

> willful killing; torture or inhuman treatment (including medical experiments; willfully causing great suffering or serious injury to body or health; extensive destruction and appropriation of property not justified by military necessity and carried out unlawfully and wantonly; compelling a prisoner of war or civilian to serve in the forces of the hostile power; willfully depriving a prisoner of war or protected civilian of the rights of a fair and regular trial; unlawful deportation or transfer of a protected civilian; unlawful confinement of a protected civilian; and taking hostages.

242

Additional Protocol I of 1977 expanded the protections of the Geneva Conventions for international conflicts to include grave breaches:

> Certain medical experimentation; making civilians and nondefended localities the object or inevitable victims of attack; the perfidious use of the Red Cross or Red Crescent emblem; transfer of an occupying power of parts of its population to occupied territory; unjustifiable delays in repatriation of prisoners of war; apartheid; attack on historic monuments; and depriving protected persons of a fair trial.

The statute of the International Criminal Tribunal for the former Yugoslavia includes "serious violations of Common Article 3 of the Geneva Conventions" (the one article that addresses civil wars), as well as other rules to protect victims of armed conflict including violence to life or health (murder, ill-treatment, torture, mutilation, corporal punishment, rape, enforced prostitution, indecent assault), summary executions, hostage taking, collective punishment, and pillage.

BIBLIOGRAPHY

References for "Exile and Return"

Timothy Garton Ash. "Anarchy & Madness." *The New York Review of Books*, February 10, 2000.

Gary Jonathan Bass. *Stay the Hand of Vengeance: The Politics of War Crimes Tribunals*. Princeton: Princeton University Press, 2000.

Roy Gutman and David Rieff (eds). *Crimes of War: What the Public Should Know*. New York: W.W. Norton & Company, 1999.

Judith Herman. *Trauma and Recovery: The Aftermath of Violence—From Domestic Abuse to Political Terror*. New York: Basic Books, 1992.

Michael Ignatieff. "Articles of Faith." *Index on Censorship 5*, 1996.

——— *Virtual War: Kosovo and Beyond*. New York: Metropolitian Books, 2000.

Sebastian Junger. "The Forensics of War." *Vanity Fair*, October 1999.

Veton Surroi. "Victims of the Victims." *The New York Review of Books*, October 7, 1999.

Human Rights Watch Reports on Kosovo

March 2000. *Kosovo: Rape as a Weapon of "Ethnic Cleansing."*

February 2000. *Civilian Deaths in the NATO Air Campaign.*

October 1999. *A Village Destroyed: War Crimes in Kosovo.*

August 1999. *Abuses Against Serbs and Roma in the New Kosovo.*

July 1999. *"Ethnic Cleansing" in the Glogovac Municipality.*

June 1999. *Ticking Time Bombs: NATO's Use of Cluster Munitions.*

March–June, 1999. *Kosovo Flashes*, nos. 1–50.

February 1999. *A Week of Terror in Drenica.*

December 1998. *Detentions and Abuse in Kosovo.*

October 1998. *Humanitarian Law Violations in Kosovo.*

December 1996. *Persecution Persists: Human Rights Violations in Kosovo.*

October 1994. *Human Rights Abuses of Non-Serbs in Kosovo, Sandzak and Vojvodina.*

March 1994. *Open Wounds: Human Rights Abuses in Kosovo.*

July 1993. *Abuses Continue in the Former Yugoslavia: Serbia, Montenegro and Bosnia-Hercegovina.*

October 1992. *Human Rights Abuses in Kosovo.*

January 1991. *Human Rights in a Dissolving Yugoslavia.*

March 1990. *Yugoslavia: Crisis in Kosovo.*

Other Reports and Sources on Kosovo

American Association for the Advancement of Science (AAAS) and the Institute for Legal and Policy Studies. *Policy or Panic? The Flight of Ethnic Albanians from Kosovo, March-May 1999*. April 2000.

American Bar Association (CEELI program) and AAAS. *Political Killings in Kosova/Kosovo*. September 2000.

American RadioWorks/Minnesota Public Radio. *Massacre at Cuska*. www.americanradioworks.org.

Amnesty International. Web page at www.amnesty.org

Balkan Human Rights. Web page at www.greekhelsinki.gr.

Bar Human Rights Committee of England and Wales. *Kosova 2000: Justice, Not Revenge*. February 2000.

Council for the Defense of Human Rights and Freedoms. Various reports available at www.albanian.com/kmdlnj.

European Roma Rights Center. *Roma in the Kosovo Conflict*. February 2000.

Helsinki Committee for Human Rights in Serbia. *Status of National Minorities in Kosovo*. May 1998.

Humanitarian Law Center. *Spotlight Reports*. 1998 and 1999.

——— *Human Rights in the Federal Republic of Yugoslavia*, 1999 Report. October 2000.

Independent International Commission on Kosovo. *The Kosovo Report*. October 2000.

International Crisis Group. *Reality Demands: Documenting Violations of International Humanitarian Law in Kosovo 1999*. June 2000.

——— *Kosovo Albanians in Serbian Prisons: Kosovo's Unfinished Business*. January 2000.

International Helsinki Federation. Various reports and statements available at www.ihf.hr.org.

International Press Institute. *The Kosovo News and Propaganda War*. September 1999.

Lawyers Committee for Human Rights. *Protection of Kosovar Refugees and Returnees: The Legal Principles*. June 1999.

——— *Kosovo: Protection and Peace-Building—Protection of Refugees, Returnees, Internally Displaced Persons, and Minorities*. August 1999.

——— *A Fragile Peace: Laying the Foundations for Justice in Kosovo*. October 1999.

Médecins Sans Frontières. *Kosovo: Accounts of a Deportation*. April 1999.

Organization for Security and Cooperation in Europe (OSCE). *Kosovo/Kosova: As Seen, As Told, Parts I and II.* December 1999.

Physicians for Human Rights. *War Crimes in Kosovo: A Population-Based Assessment of Human Rights Violations Against Kosovar Albanians.* August 1999.

Society for Threatened Peoples. Kosovo: *War, Expulsion, Massacres.* August 1998.

United Nations High Commissioner for Refugees and OSCE. *Assessments of the Situation of Ethnic Minorities in Kosovo.* July 1999, November 1999, February 2000, and June 2000.

United Nations Special Rapporteur on the Situation of Human Rights in Bosnia and Herzegovina, the Republic of Croatia and the Federal Republic of Yugoslavia. *Periodic Report on the Situation of Human Rights in Bosnia and Herzegovina, the Republic of Croatia and the Federal Republic of Yugoslavia,* September 24, 1999; Addendum, November 1, 1999.

United States Department of State, *Erasing History: Ethnic Cleansing in Kosovo.* May 1999.

———— *Ethnic Cleansing—An Accounting.* December 1999.

———— *Kosovo Judicial Assessment Mission Report.* April 2000.

Chain of Command Sources

Policajac Magazine (Serbian Ministry of Internal Affairs)

Vojska Magazine (Yugoslav Army)

Serbian Ministry of Internal Affairs Website (www.mup.sr.gov.yu/domino\mup.nsf/pages/index-e, as of May 18, 2001)

Nedeljni Telegraf newspaper

Nasa Borba newspaper

Politika newspaper

Evropljanin newspaper

Vecernje Novosti newspaper

vreme Magazine

Beta News Agency

Tanjug News Agency

Radio B-92

OSCE. *Kosovo/Kosova: As Seen, As Told, Part 1.* (www.osce.org/kosovo/reports/hr/part1/ch3.htm)

Federation of American Scientists website (www.fas.org/man/dod-101/ops/kosovo.htm)

United Kingdom Ministry of Defense website (www.kosovo.mod.uk/mupstruct.htm)

Jane's Defense Weekly website (www.janes.com/regional_news/europe/news/kosovo/jwa9904 01_01_n.shtml)

American RadioWorks, *Massacre at Cuska* (www.americanradioworks.org/features/kosovo/index.htm)

International Crisis Group, *Reality Demands* (www.intl-crisis-group.org/projects/showreport.cfm /reportid=57)

Frontline, *War in Europe* (www.pbs.org/wgbh/pages/frontline/shows/kosovo/)

CONTRIBUTORS

Fred Abrahams was the Human Rights Watch researcher covering the southern Balkans from 1995 to 2000. During that time, he published numerous articles and reports on human rights and humanitarian law in Albania, Macedonia, and Kosovo. He is currently a fellow at the Open Society Institute writing a book about Albania's transition to democracy.

Carroll Bogert is the communications director at Human Rights Watch. She spent eleven years as a foreign correspondent for *Newsweek* magazine, based in Beijing, Southeast Asia, and the former Soviet Union. She is the author, with Liu Heung-shing, of *USSR: The Collapse of an Empire*.

Gilles Peress is a photographer with *The New Yorker* and Senior Research Associate with the Human Rights Center at the University of California, Berkeley. He has been with Magnum Photos since 1971. His photographs are exhibited in and collected by the Metropolitan Museum of Art, New York; Museum of Modern Art, New York; the Chicago Art Institute; and the Minneapolis Institute of Art, among others. Peress' books include *Telex Iran*; *The Silence*; *Farewell to Bosnia*; and *The Graves: Srebrenica and Vukovar*.

Eric Stover is Director of the Human Rights Center and Adjunct Professor of Public Health at the University of California, Berkeley. His books include *The Breaking of Bodies and Minds: Torture, Psychiatric Abuse, and the Health Professions* (with Elena O. Nightingale); *Witnesses from the Grave: The Stories Bones Tell* (with Christopher Joyce); and *The Graves: Srebrenica and Vukovar*.

Jeff Streeper has designed *Vietnam: The Land We Never Knew* by Geoffrey Clifford; *Annie Leibovitz 1970–1990* by Annie Leibovitz; *A Simpler Way* by Margaret J. Wheatley and Myron Kellner-Rogers; and *Crimes of War: What the Public Should Know* edited by Roy Gutman and David Rieff.

ACKNOWLEDGMENTS

This book would not have been possible without the cooperation of the villagers around Pec, who recounted horrific events in the hope that perpetrators will be brought to justice. This book is dedicated to them.

This book is also dedicated to the memory of Kurt Schork, a courageous and compassionate journalist who covered the wars in Bosnia and Kosovo and died during an ambush in Sierra Leone on May 24, 2000.

Many other individuals provided invaluable assistance to the project. The family of Flamur Kelmendi, especially his son Adriatik, provided translation, expert advice, and, despite the destruction of their own home, gracious housing. Michael Montgomery and Stephen Smith of American RadioWorks were essential collaborators, whose skills as journalists greatly assisted the research. Their radio documentaries on Cuska are among the best reporting from the war in Kosovo.

The Pec office of the Council for the Defense of Human Rights and Freedoms provided valuable information, as did the Pec municipal office. As always, the Humanitarian Law Center and its director, Natasa Kandic, were a great assistance. Gillian Caldwell from the Witness Project of the Lawyers Committee for Human Rights kindly provided material recorded in the Cuska area.

The Open Society Institute and The Sandler Family Supporting Foundation generously provided funding to the Human Rights Center for the production of this book. Jonathan Cobb edited Eric Stover's essay "Exile and Return," portions of which first appeared, in French, in Remy Ourdan, ed., *Apres Guerre(s)* (Paris: Autrement, 2001). Eric Stover and science writer Christopher Joyce jointly interviewed Qamil Shehu and Graham Blewitt while on assignment with National Public Radio.

In the production process, many people played important roles. Cate Fallon, Jeff Ladd, Elizabeth Sasser, and Canace Pulfer at the Gilles Peress Studio contributed their time and expertise. At Human Rights Watch, technical and administrative support came from Alex Frangos, Veronica Matushaj, Rachel Bien, and Alexandra Perina. The director of the Europe and Central Asia Division, Holly Cartner, oversaw the entire Kosovo work. Dinah PoKempner, Human Rights Watch General Counsel, provided a legal review. Special thanks go to Craig Bloom and Jeremy Feigelson of the law firm Debevoise & Plimpton for pro-bono legal services related to this work; Jeffrey Posternak and Tracy Bohan of the Wylie Agency; and Rachel Shigekane at the Human Rights Center.

Human Rights Watch
Europe and Central Asia Division

Human Rights Watch is dedicated to protecting the human rights of people around the world.

We stand with victims and activists to bring offenders to justice, to prevent discrimination, to uphold political freedom and to protect people from inhumane conduct in wartime.

We investigate and expose human rights violations and hold abusers accountable.

We challenge governments and those holding power to end abusive practices and respect international human rights law.

We enlist the public and the international community to support the cause of human rights for all.

http://www.hrw.org

Human Rights Center
University of California, Berkeley

Established through the generosity of The Sandler Family Supporting Foundation, the Human Rights Center conducts interdisciplinary research on emerging issues in international human rights and humanitarian law. Our research focuses on war crimes, the role of justice and accountability in the aftermath of genocide and other forms of mass violence, health and human rights, and refugees.

We believe that the academy can inform the work of practitioners, while activists and other professionals can influence the direction of human rights research in the university. Because creativity and leadership are essential to the human rights movement, we seek out and support graduate students and professionals who are making or could potentially make significant contributions to the promotion and protection of human rights in the United States and abroad.

The Human Rights Center brings together photographers, writers, artists, and students to design books and create websites and exhibitions in an effort to focus public attention on unfolding human rights crises. The Human Rights Watch/ Human Rights Center publication, *A Village Destroyed: May 14, 1999: War Crimes in Kosovo*, is a product of that effort.

http://hrcberkeley.org

Milosevic Arrested

On April 1, 2001, five months after his fall from power, Slobodan Milosevic surrendered to Serbian authorities and was taken to Belgrade's Central Prison where he faced charges of financial irregularities, misusing customs duties, abusing his powers and causing "damage to the Serbian economy." A month later, a Belgrade court delivered the Tribunal's indictment for war crimes to Milosevic in his jail cell. He refused to accept the document and it was left on the bars of his cell.

On May 25, a new twist developed in the Milosevic case when the Serbian police announced that the former president had tried to cover up atrocities in Kosovo, including the dumping of bodies in the Danube River. The new allegations came after police investigated reports that a truck containing 50 bodies, reportedly those of ethnic Albanians, was discovered in the Danube River outside Kosovo near the Romanian border in April 1999.

Police captain Dragan Kareusa told reporters that the bodies discovered in the truck were reloaded and buried in another location. He went on to reveal that in a March 1999

meeting, Milosevic ordered top police commanders "to remove all evidence" of civilian casualties during the war in Kosovo and to remove corpses that could be subject to "possible investigation by the Hague Tribunal."

In the evening of June 28, with billions of dollars in international aid hanging in the balance, the Serbian authorities handed Milosevic over to the Hague Tribunal. His departure coincided with Vidovdan, the anniversary of the battle of Kosovo in 1389 and perhaps the most important date in the Serbian calendar. A bitter irony of his transfer was that it was made by men from the most feared unit that Milosevic himself had created—the Special Operations Unit (JSO).

According to *The Sunday Times* of London, at exactly 6:17 pm JSO agents placed Milosevic in a black Chrysler, which left the prison following a special forces Mercedes with blacked-out windows and a Citroen van. As the convoy swept on to a runway at the Belgrade airport, a JSO helicopter landed and three officials from the Hague Tribunal escorted Milosevic onto the helicopter. He was then taken to an American army base in Tuzla, Bosnia. From there, he was flown to the Scheveningen detention center in The Hague.

Dressed smartly in a dark suit, Milosevic appeared before the war crimes tribunal on July 3. Refusing legal counsel, he sought to turn the arraignment into an attack on the court's legitimacy and on NATO for its bombing of Serbia. "I consider this tribunal a false tribunal and indictments false indictments", he said in English.

Judge Richard May of Britain asked Milosevic whether he would like to have the indictment against him read aloud or whether he would waive that right, to which the former Yugoslav president snapped back: "That's your problem."

When asked if he wished to enter a guilty or not guilty plea, Milosevic replied in Serbian: "This tribunal's aim is to produce false justification for the war crimes committed by NATO against Yugoslavia." Judge May again asked if Milosevic wished to enter a plea, and he responded: "I have given you my answer. Furthermore, this so-called tribunal..." Switching off Milosevic's microphone, Judge May said, "Mr.

Milosevic, we treat your response as a failure to enter a plea and we shall enter pleas of not guilty on each count on your behalf."

Three times during the 12-minute proceedings, Judge May cut off Milosevic in midsentence, once commenting, "Mr. Milosevic, this is not the time for speeches."

On November 16, Judge May issued a sweeping new indictment against Milosevic, charging him with genocide in connection with the war in Bosnia-Herzegovina in 1992-95. Two previous indictments had accused the former Yugoslav president of commiting crimes against humanity and grave breaches of the Geneva Conventions. This new indictment makes Milosevic the first head of state to stand trial for what is considered the most heinous of all state-sponsored crimes.

—Eric Stover - November 24, 2001